GREAT LIVES

Francis Drake

OVERLEAF LEFT Sir Francis Drake,
who won the admiration of the
English for his devoted service to
Elizabeth I.

OVERLEAF RIGHT A miniature of
Drake painted by Nicholas Hilliard

GREAT LIVES

Francis Drake

Neville Williams

Introduction by Elizabeth Longford

Weidenfeld and Nicolson London

For my godson Stuart Rackham

© George Weidenfeld and Nicolson Limited
and Book Club Associates 1973

All rights reserved. No part
of this publication may be
reproduced, stored in a
retrieval system, or trans-
mitted, in any form or by any
means, electronic, mechanical,
photocopying or otherwise,
without the prior permission
of the copyright owner.

House editor Jenny Ashby
Art editor Andrew Shoolbred
Layout by Margaret Downing

Filmset by Keyspools Ltd, Golborne, Lancashire
Printed Offset-Litho by Cox & Wyman Ltd
London, Fakenham and Reading

Contents

Introduction 7
Preface 9
1 The Protestant Wind 12
2 Slaving and the Spanish Main 32
3 The Treasure House of the World 55
4 The World Encompassed 80
5 Corsair Extraordinary 120
6 Singeing the King of Spain's Beard 148
7 The Armada and After 168
8 The Sun's Fellow Traveller 206
Further Reading 227
List of Illustrations 228
Index 231

Introduction

CERTAIN THINGS will always serve to heighten the English awareness of nationhood: the historical plays of Shakespeare, for instance, or Churchill's war-time speeches. The voyages and victories of Sir Francis Drake did more than heighten the national consciousness; they created it. At a time of great exuberance overseas, life in these rather remote islands could easily have drifted off into the void. Thanks to Drake, England butted her way into the limelight. Foreign princes and ambassadors wondered nervously what he would be up to next. The peoples of the Iberian Peninsula spoke of that devil, 'El Draque', with bated breath.

Drake's life, like all great sagas, has more than one facet. First, it is a romance of the sea, high-lighted by the epic voyage of the *Golden Hind* round the world. For Drake, the moment of truth had come when he sighted the Pacific and uttered his prayer that Almighty God in his goodness 'would give me life and leave to sail once in an English bottom upon that sea'. John Oxenham, his companion, added a fervent 'Amen'. But the Almighty, in his mysterious goodness, saw fit to deliver Oxenham into the hands of the Spanish Inquisition.

This brings us to the next facet: Drake's passionate devotion to the reformed religion. Not without reason does Neville Williams entitle his opening chapter 'The Protestant Wind'. But though it was a Protestant gale of faith which inspired Drake's whole career and was said to have blown away the Armada, Drake had plenty of rumbustious worldliness to match a materialistic age. One likes to hear that he was a strongly made, stocky sea-dog with a blond beard. The physique of the *Golden Hind* seemed to echo her captain's: she was 'very stout and very strong ... staunch'. Sometimes bombastic and always master of the highest tone, Drake was what Dr Williams aptly calls 'a high privateer' – a privateer on the grand scale, operating on the high seas, not merely in the Channel or along the coasts.

Here indeed is a more challenging aspect of the story. How far did Drake's poverty as a boy excuse his lust for prize-money? Or was there no need for excuses in the sixteenth century, on the Spanish Main? Yet even in those days there were Englishmen as well as Spaniards who labelled him 'a vile corsair', a man capable of going after a prize-ship when the Armada was already spending its second night in the Channel. Queen Elizabeth, nevertheless, spoke of him lovingly as her 'pirate'. She was his most important shareholder. Later, out of the proceeds, she was able to make substantial investments in the Levant, from which grew the East India Company, and so the Indian Empire of her descendant Queen Victoria. From Drake's drum to the Delhi Durbars – no mean sequence. Nor was it entirely due to the plunder-motive, which after all had been forced on Drake when Spain designated the New World a closed market. It was his magnetic leadership which was responsible for much of the success and most of the glory.

His leadership is the final facet. If his discipline could be harsh, he applied it all round. 'I must have the gentleman to haul and draw with the mariner', he insisted, 'and the mariner with the gentleman. . . .' On his last voyage there were so many volunteers that the press gang went out of business. Drake's life bears all the imprints of heroism in a national context: especially self-confidence, audacity, good fortune and a gift for command which made him feared but also deeply loved.

Elizabeth Longford

Preface

To write a short account of one of the most remarkable men of action of all times is rather like attempting to cram the crown jewels into a matchbox. In the following pages, accordingly, I have concentrated on Drake's principal achievements which affected the mainstream of English history, but I have also been at pains to portray him as a child of his generation. A work of this kind is necessarily grounded on the contributions of a long line of maritime historians. I wish to pay tribute here not to any particular individual, but to the work of three great institutions – the Navy Records Society, the Hakluyt Society and the Society for Nautical Research.

I am much indebted both to Elizabeth, Lady Longford, general editor of this new series of biographies, and to Christopher Falkus of George Weidenfeld and Nicolson Ltd, for their personal encouragement to me while preparing this life of Sir Francis Drake. In the later stages of production I have been most grateful to John Curtis and Jenny Ashby for their valuable assistance. The book owes much to David Brinson for his skilful selection of the illustrations. Once again it is a pleasure to thank Annabel Clover for typing my manuscript, and to record my lively appreciation to my wife for her unfailing support.

NW
London 17 May 1973

1
The Protestant Wind

PREVIOUS PAGES Edward VI at the deathbed of his father Henry VIII. The presence of the Pope in the foreground of this painting symbolizes the clash between Catholicism and Protestantism during the reigns of the Tudors which formed the backcloth to Drake's life.

A contemporary engraving of Drake.

FRANCIS DRAKE is in the first flight of England's national heroes. Like the Queen whom he served so devotedly, he was a child of the English Reformation. Wrenched from his native Devonshire at a tender age, as a direct result of his father's religious views, he was brought up in near poverty and had from his earliest years to make his own way in a harsh, competitive world. Despite these drawbacks, he was indeed fortunate in the age in which he lived. The profession of mariner on which he embarked, more by force of circumstance than from deliberate choice, brought him in due course to play a role on the international stage on which the conflict between England and Spain was being acted out, and he soon came to dominate that stage as the principal actor. Had he been born a century earlier, he would no doubt have lived a busy but uneventful life as a relatively unknown shipmaster, indulging in privateering in the Channel and serving his country at sea in the days of an *ad hoc* navy during the wars with France, but nonetheless remote from politics and a stranger to the royal Court. Yet in the century of the Reformation, with Europe's horizons expanding and nationalism hardening, a seaman of his calibre was able by strength of character and sheer professional ability to acquire a world-wide reputation. Drake had the good fortune to be thoroughly attuned to his age as circumnavigator, high privateer and the embodiment of England's sea power, in days when, out of the crucible of the struggle with the Colossus of Spain, the people of England were being forged into a nation. The last quarter of the sixteenth century was, accordingly, as much the era of Drake as it was the Elizabethan age.

The Drakes had been settled in Devon for centuries and one branch of the family had farmed lands in the Tavistock area without a break from the mid-fourteenth century. Over the generations, they played their part in the administration of the borough of Tavistock; some younger sons became monks at St Rumon's Abbey, others turned to Plymouth and the seas for their livelihood. On the southern edge of Dartmoor, Tavistock was fifteen miles due north of Plymouth and slightly nearer Launceston, the county town of Cornwall. It was a key town on the main road to Liskeard, Bodmin and the far south-west and also commanded the least inhospitable of the routes crossing Dartmoor to Ashburton and thence to Exeter and the London road. It was a place of some consequence, quite apart from the great Benedictine Abbey of St Rumon, for Tavistock enjoyed privileges as one of the

John, Lord Russell, whose son Francis stood sponsor for Drake, born in the vicinity of the Russell lands around Tavistock Abbey.

four stannary towns, where the tin mined in Cornwall and west Devon was assayed and stamped; it returned two members to Parliament and it held, by royal charter, a three-day fair each year at which 'Devonshire dozens', woven in neighbouring hamlets from the wool produced by the Dartmoor flocks, were bought by clothiers. The River Tavy, rushing down from the moors, flowed south, passing Buckland Abbey to join the Tamar and then the open sea. Tavistock was, in short, very far from being an isolated borough.

John Drake of Crowndale near Tavistock and his wife Margery Hawkins had four sons, of whom the second, Edmund, began life as a sailor. Tradition has it that his travels to the ports of northern

Drake's Protestant Background

Drake was born into a Devon family which had played an active part in the administrative and religious life of the Tavistock area. His father, rumour had it, became a convert to Protestantism as a result of his travels as a sailor to the ports of northern Europe. Drake's early childhood was spent as a refugee when his family fled from Crowndale during the Prayer Book Rebellion. The map above shows the town of Plymouth and it's environs, including St Nicolas's Ireland, later named after the national hero.

ABOVE RIGHT John Fox, the Protestant martyrologist whose writings remain as a memorial to the struggles of the early Protestants.
RIGHT Sir Thomas Wyatt, the younger, leader of the Kentish rebellion designed to avert the calamity of a marriage between Queen Elizabeth and the Catholic Philip II of Spain.

Europe led to his conversion to the Protestant faith. By 1542, however, Edmund Drake had left the sea to settle down in a cottage on his father's farm and to be taken on by Lord Russell as a shearman. About that time, he married a local girl and a few years afterwards – possibly as late as 1544 – the eldest of their twelve sons, Francis, was born at his grandfather's house at Crowndale. Francis Russell, son of John, Lord Russell, the new owner of Tavistock Abbey, stood sponsor for the child, who was given his Christian name. Events were to force Edmund Drake and his young family far from their native Devon, but Francis would return in glory to the county, still under forty – a national hero, knighted by his sovereign and wealthy enough to become owner of Buckland Abbey no more than six miles south of the humble farmhouse in which he had been born.

Those were troubled years in the Devonshire countryside and this turbulence was matched by lawlessness at sea. In 1538 the greatest landowner of the west, Henry Courtenay, Earl of Devon and Marquess of Exeter, had fallen through conspiring with the Pole family, who were too near the throne for the King's comfort, and Courtenay's execution and the confiscation of his estates sent tremors throughout the county. Within a year, Tavistock Abbey had surrendered to the Crown, and its buildings and considerable properties were granted to Lord Russell, recently ennobled after thirty years of loyal service to King Henry as diplomat, soldier and household official; he had lost an eye at the battle of Morlaix and in 1540 was to become Lord High Admiral. Century-old traditions were crumbling and the future seemed uncertain. The monks who had dispensed regular charity at the gates of St Rumon's Abbey were now beggars themselves. However, the Drakes of Crowndale Farm by the Tavy, as ardent followers of the reformed faith, welcomed their new lay landlords, whose outlook they shared; it was, surely, unusual for a peer's son to stand as godfather to a yeoman's grandson. When John, Lord Russell, by now Lord Privy Seal, came down to Devon from Court, men eagerly quizzed him, given the chance, to learn the latest news. King Henry, a swollen giant of a man, was in constant pain with his leg, while the indiscreet prophesied his death and enemies of his rule whispered that he had already died. Who would win the duel in Council between the Howards and the Seymours for wielding supreme power when the boy Edward should inherit the crown? John and Edmund Drake would have been more interested in hearing news about the feud which Stephen Gardiner, Bishop of

Winchester, waged with Archbishop Cranmer to capture the King's conscience; for the Bishop to triumph would spell religious reaction that not a few neighbours in Tavistock would applaud, and since the burning of Anne Askewe for heresy no man or woman of advanced views, such as the Drakes professed, could feel safe.

There was clearly relief at Crowndale when, on King Henry's death at the beginning of 1547, Edward Seymour, Earl of Hertford, seized power as Lord Protector and retained Lord Russell as a key councillor. The future seemed assured, and yet the undercurrent of unrest in the West Country that had existed ever since the fall of the abbeys became more pronounced with the radical religious changes that came with Protector Somerset's rule. It would not take much to set Devon and Cornwall aflame. In 1548 there was a serious riot at Helston, and one of the Cornish rebels was hanged on Plymouth Hoe. To bring home to people the enormity of disobedience to the edicts of Church and state, the body of the traitor, quartered after hanging, was distributed to neighbouring towns so that the men of Tavistock received a gruesome reminder of the penalties paid by traitors, as they passed the gibbet in the market-place. Next year there was a much greater threat to the new order, with local reaction to the dissolution of the chantries, and fears about the new liturgy. King Edward's English Prayer Book was to come into force on Whit Sunday, and while the Drakes quickly rejoiced that the true Gospel which they had followed, even in days when some would have branded them heretics, would at last become the established religion of the entire realm, others planned to demonstrate in favour of the old Mass of King Henry's day and to demand the re-enactment of the Act of Six Articles which enshrined Catholic doctrine and the ancient ceremonies. The Prayer Book Rebellion, as it was called, originated in Bodmin, but it spread swiftly throughout Cornwall and into Devon. In Tavistock itself, John Prideaux was in the forefront of those determined to put back the clock to the Latin service, the ancient ritual, the veneration of relics, the confessional and the days of the monks.

Not only was the English Bible overthrown but barns were burned. For so obvious a sympathizer with the new order, it was too dangerous for Edmund Drake to remain at Crowndale. His protector, Lord Russell, was away in London on the King's business and it would be many days before he could reach Devon with an army. Drake decided to abandon his cottage and small-

A map of the world as it was known at the beginning of the fifteenth century, before any of the great discoveries had been made. It is taken from the Santeram Facsimile Atlas printed in 1849.

holding and leave with his wife and young family, so Francis, not yet five years old, found himself a refugee. They first made for Plymouth where no doubt they hoped to find safety with their Hawkins kin, but Plymouth had surrendered to the insurgents through the Mayor's treachery, and in the fighting a distant relative, John Drake, who had been Receiver of the city the previous year, was shot through both cheeks by an arrow. A number of fervent Protestants took refuge on St Nicholas's Island in the Sound and they may have included the Drakes. (Years afterwards, it was by the island that Sir Francis would anchor the *Golden Hind* after his circumnavigation of the world, which aroused Devonians to change the name from St Nicholas's to 'Drake's Island'.) It was not until 9 August that Lord Russell took Exeter and stamped out the last embers of rebellion with severity. Meanwhile, a squadron of the King's ships under Vice-Admiral Sir Thomas Cotton, which had been fitted out to clear the English Channel of pirates, had been ordered to Plymouth to relieve the city, and the expedition included a Captain Richard Drake, who was a native of Plymouth.

Edmund Drake and his family are next discovered living in a hulk near Gillingham on the River Medway. It seems most likely that Edmund, having decided that there was no future in trying to return to Crowndale, persuaded Richard Drake or another captain to give them a passage. The journey by land would have been far more difficult. Edmund's father had much more to lose by flight and was clearly a trimmer in religion compared with his son; he stayed on unmolested at Crowndale as a tenant of the Russells until his death in 1566.

In the mid-sixteenth century, the seas were as lawless as at any time in the last four hundred years, giving men bold enough to take risks opportunities for rich plunder. Henry VIII's final war with France unleashed an intensive bout of privateering in the English Channel, which heartened the Hawkins family of Plymouth. In 1545 an English captain, Robert Reneger from Southampton, astonished the Courts of Europe by despoiling a Spanish treasure ship on its way home from the Indies. Trade with Spain was at this time being hampered by all kinds of restrictions, and English merchants in San Sebastian and other ports were being brought before the Inquisition; a Londoner had even been burned at the stake there as a heretic. Reneger had lawfully taken a French ship according to the rules of warfare but had brought her into a Spanish harbour, where the prize was impounded, and when he was unable to obtain satisfaction from the intransigent authorities, he sailed out of port bent on revenge. He had picked up news that the *San Salvador* was returning to Spain from Hispaniola with a valuable cargo and he went in search of her. Ten leagues off Cape St Vincent, Reneger bore down on his prey and robbed her of much gold, 124 chests of sugar and 140 hides, worth altogether 7,243,075 *maravedis*.

Back in England, Reneger wisely reported the affair to the Privy Council, for he sensed the importance of his *coup*, and the Council, including Lord Russell, ordered that the bullion be lodged in the Tower of London. The Spanish ambassador pressed for his punishment 'in exemplary fashion, as a pirate', yet Captain Reneger was given a wonderful reception at Court 'for his fine

OVERLEAF Martin Behaim's maps of the world, divided into its eastern and western hemispheres. Taken from a globe constructed in 1492, they are printed here, in translation from the German, in the American Lippincott's Geographical Series published in 1864, and show the increased knowledge which the fifteenth century brought to explorers and geographers.

piece of work ... and swaggers about everywhere', as the ambassador reported, almost in tears; though it were 'far better for everyone if he [Reneger] took up another profession', Henry VIII promptly appointed him to a command in his fleet. The bullion in the Tower was not returned to Spain for another eight years, after interminable haggling, and then it was no more than a

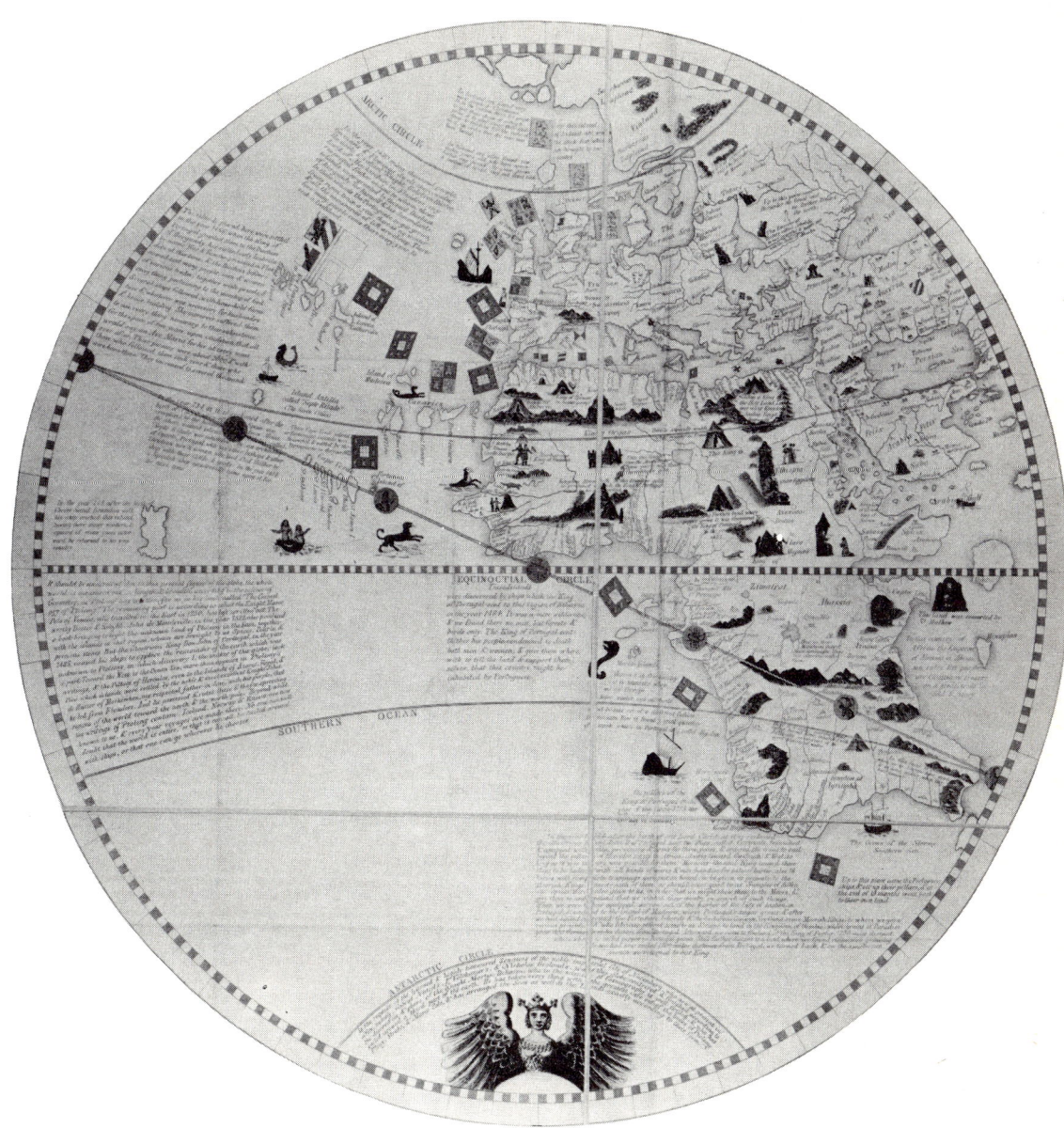

third of the sum originally claimed, so that Reneger was left with a vast fortune. He retired from the seas to end his days peaceably as a customs official in Southampton. His attack on the *San Salvador* in Drake's infancy opened a new chapter in the history of prizes at sea. Inspired by his adventure, numbers of West Countrymen took to more systematic plundering of Spanish shipping, yet until Drake's prime, Reneger's success was never to be approached. There were to be forty years of uneasy truce during which there was an unbroken series of incidents on the high seas in which the maritime power of Spain was seriously challenged, and when Francis Drake attacked Philip II's Plate Fleet, it was to the Reneger affair that both the English and the Spanish Courts turned for precedent. In a very striking sense, Francis had been born under Robert Reneger's star.

It was hard for the boy Francis to understand why his family had had to leave Crowndale. The voyage to the Medway from Plymouth was an adventure beyond his wildest dreams and at the end of it there was the excitement of their makeshift home in the hull of an old ship moored on the river. This was the only accommodation the Drakes could find and it was to be their abode for several years, for we are told that several of Edmund's children were born there. (Of Francis's eleven brothers, we know the names of only four – Edward who died in his teens, John and Joseph who both perished in the expedition to Nombre de Dios and Thomas, the baby of the family. It would have been unusual if this large family included no girl.) At Gillingham Reach, below Chatham, a new naval base was being established and, perhaps through Lord Russell's influence, Edmund obtained the post of chaplain, administering to the spiritual needs of the seamen from the King's ships anchored off the reach. His experiences at Crowndale had intensified his fervour to preach the word, and his forthright evangelism made up for his lack of formal training.

Young Francis was short for his age, and this was quite an advantage in living afloat, where hatches and low beams were hazards for the tall; before he was thirty, he would be rather stocky. He had brown hair and blue eyes and would never lose his Devonian speech. He had no schooling, but learned to read and write from his father, who instructed his children in the rudiments of Protestant doctrine. 'Make the most of the Bible', the old man wrote at his end to Thomas, his youngest son. The boys must sometimes have heard their father reading the Scriptures aloud to seamen and leading prayers, and it would have delighted Edmund had he known that during his commands Francis preached fervently, is recorded as having converted a Welsh seaman and often had to fill a pastoral role in comforting men dying of disease or wounds.

Mrs Drake is a shadowy figure and we do not know her name.

She had been forced to exchange the security of a cottage on the Russell estate for a hulk on the Medway, where she was a complete stranger, never seeing her Devonshire relatives again. For a time, she and her husband lived in poverty. Busy with her growing family, she became worn out by childbearing and had died before Edmund was presented to a living and moved into a solidly built vicarage.

Living on the water amidst the King's ships made Francis determined to follow a career at sea, as his father had in his bachelor days. At Gillingham there was salt in the air and a smell of pitch. He picked up much nautical lore – about winds and tides, cordage and sails, soundings and ballast and the other strands of seamanship. A boy on a hulk could not avoid mastering the problems of splicing, and the Medway was a wonderful place for watching the ways in which seasoned captains furled their sails and weighed anchor. The poverty of those early years also had its effect as Drake grew to manhood. He was sent off to earn a living as soon as he was able and this meant an early apprenticeship as a boy seaman. In years to come, he was always fascinated by the thought of treasure, for a successful prize could turn an everyday ship's captain into a man of great substance overnight, as Robert Reneger had shown.

Four years after the Drakes left Devon, King Edward VI died and Northumberland's desperate attempt to set aside the true succession, in which Lord Russell, now Earl of Bedford, and his son, Drake's godfather, were involved, foundered. The Catholic Mary became Queen of England and Edmund Drake could no longer expect to retain his naval chaplaincy. In January 1554 Sir Thomas Wyatt of Kent led a rebellion to prevent the Queen from marrying Philip of Spain and it was from ships on the Medway that Wyatt secretly obtained armaments; at one stage, too, the rebels attacked the royal fleet moored at Gillingham. The Catholic reaction was far more serious for the Drakes than the Prayer Book rising had been, for with Wyatt's defeat the government was firmly established and persecution of Protestants became a norm of policy. Many reformists, clergy and laity, fled abroad to Zurich and Geneva to tarry for better times, but Edmund Drake stayed in Kent and through discretion avoided disaster. He disappears from view until January 1561 when, as a clerk in holy orders, he was instituted by Archbishop Parker to the vicarage of Upchurch near Gillingham.

Mary's marriage to Philip of Spain and the subordination of

English interests to Spanish policy, as much as the Queen's rigid Catholicism which produced martyrs at Smithfield, Oxford and elsewhere, provoked a nationalist reaction on Elizabeth's accession. It was Philip, men swore, who had lost England her last Continental outpost – Calais, the remnant of a great dominion in France – so that the realm had shrunk to the size it was in the days of King Harold, while Spain developed her empire in the Americas. English seamen regarded their native land as a David that would slay the Spanish Goliath; and while many of them justified their depredations in the New World on nationalist, political grounds no less than from sheer commercial prudence, Drake himself never played down the religious issues. His family's flight from Devonshire and the aftermath of Wyatt's rebellion had made him an unquestioning follower of his father's teaching, so that he came to oppose King Philip's subjects not just for being Spaniards, but for professing Catholicism as well.

From about the age of ten, soon after Wyatt's rebellion, Francis was placed with 'a neighbouring pilot' (as he later told the chronicler William Camden), who 'by daily exercise hardened him to the sailor's labour with a little bark, wherewith he sailed up and down the coast, guided ships in and out of harbours and sometimes transported merchandise to France and Zeeland'. Pilotage in the Thames approaches and the Medway was a highly skilled affair and so the boy had a marvellous opportunity of learning from an old hand. Then there was the thrill of crossing the narrow seas to come alongside in a foreign port and be involved in the bustle of unloading, and dealing with customs officials and with merchants on the quays. A lad had to be quick-witted and nimble to survive the cut and thrust of visits to Fécamp and Flushing where, because he was an inexperienced youngster, he would be an obvious target for cheats and pranksters. These little barks of ten tons' burthen were maids of all work along the south-east coast. They spent most of their time carrying food for London's larder, bringing corn from Faversham, butter and cheese from Ipswich and herrings from Yarmouth, though most of these trades were seasonal. If the owner was fortunate, they would load at London with a range of miscellaneous goods coming from the city markets and bound for provincial ports – pots and pans, dyes for the cloth trade, nails, feather-beds, indeed almost everything from vinegar to brown paper.

Pamphleteers always claimed that the coasting-trade was the 'nursery of English seamen' and in Drake's case it was certainly

OPPOSITE Mary as Queen, with her Catholic consort Philip II of Spain. During her short reign numbers of Protestants were burned as heretics; many more left England.

Drake's Predecessors in the World of Reconnaissance

The fifteenth century was a time of exploration and discovery and opened up all the major possibilities which later seafarers were to exploit. Columbus discovered America in 1492 while much earlier the Portuguese Henry the Navigator had financed a number of voyages in the Atlantic. Increasing technical and geographical expertise helped explorers, and the gap between actual achievement and its record on contemporary maps narrowed.

ABOVE Nicholas Copernicus, whose astronomical research was vital to the sixteenth-century explorers.
RIGHT Vasco da Gama, whose efforts to destroy the Arab monopoly on the spice trade by finding a new route to the spice islands foreshadowed the journeys of Magellan (1519–20).
FAR RIGHT The Portuguese explorer Ferdinand Magellan. Drake to some extent built on his discoveries and rounded the South American coast by way of Magellan's Strait.

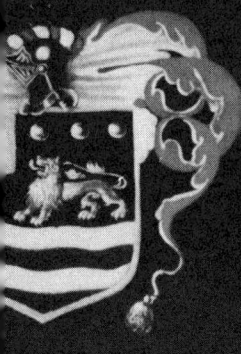

ÆTATIS SVÆ LVIII
Ano Dñi 1591

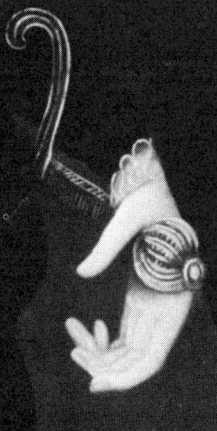

true; from small beginnings along the south-east coast with an occasional trip across the Channel, he graduated to ocean voyages and the hazards of deep-sea navigation. Calais, until its loss in 1558, was reserved for the Merchants of the Staple, but Drake's bark sometimes visited Boulogne and Fécamp in peacetime with consignments of cloth, leather and the quantities of 'old shoes' for which there was a ready market in France, and it would return with wine and canvas. More frequent were the trips to the Netherland harbours of Flushing, Dordrecht, Haarlem and especially Antwerp, the great international port. Here his bark would be laden with hops and sugar, Burgundy glass and straw hats, prunes, paper, spectacles, combs and, now and again, some packs with damask and taffeta or a chest with Venetian lutes. Antwerp, the pearl of the old Burgundian dominion, had passed with the rest of the Netherlands to Spanish control, but soon Philip II would be involved in a lengthy struggle to preserve his inheritance, and in the Dutch War of Independence, Antwerp would twice be sacked. England's war at sea against the Spaniards, that was to be epitomized by Drake's career, ensured that London would succeed Antwerp as the entrepôt of world trade.

During Mary's reign, Drake found his sea legs. The old pilot was so impressed by his diligence and skill afloat that when he died childless early in the new reign, about the same time that Edmund Drake was becoming Vicar of Upchurch, he left Francis his vessel. At seventeen, then, Francis had a command of his own and was a master-owner in his own right, small though the craft was. It was a tremendous change in his fortunes. With the bark as his capital, he continued for a few years earning as much as he could from the coasting trade and trips across to the Netherlands until he felt that he was ready for more distant ventures. His apprenticeship was over and after a voyage to Spain as a purser, or third officer, in a larger vessel, he decided to sell his bark and return to his native Devon to seek employment with his cousin John Hawkins of Plymouth, ten years his senior and already a man with a reputation in London for being a pioneering merchant adventurer. This was to be the turning-point in Drake's career.

OPPOSITE Sir John Hawkins, a native of Plymouth and cousin of Drake. To him Drake owed his early experience as a sailor and his first taste of the rich promise of the New World, which he was later so successfully to plunder for his Queen.

2
Slaving and the Spanish Main

SOME TIME DURING 1564, the year after John Hawkins had returned from his first slaving voyage between Sierra Leone and San Domingo, infringing in turn the trading monopoly of the Portuguese in West Africa and that of the Spanish in America, Francis Drake came to settle in Plymouth, to join his cousin as a very junior partner in the thriving Hawkins family business. Though Hawkins had run into trouble when two of his ships were seized as smugglers at Seville, he still made a very handsome profit on this, his first Atlantic voyage. The news of John's venture had spread to the Medway and fascinated the young mariner, who felt proud to be related to him. This, he was convinced, was only the first of many such trading voyages to the New World, and he wanted to play a part in this enterprise himself and stake a modest claim of his own to the profits it would surely bring. According to the chronicler William Camden, Drake did not journey alone, for, learning about fresh preparations which Hawkins was making 'for the voyage of America, which was called the New World, he made sale of his bark and accompanied with certain brave and able mariners he left Kent' to join his relatives in Plymouth.

At this time, the Hawkins family symbolized Plymouth, just as Plymouth itself was, under the new Queen, becoming synonymous with the re-orientation of England's maritime enterprise, much as Bristol had been sixty years earlier. Old William Hawkins, the real founder of the family's fortunes, had made privateering voyages to Guinea and to Brazil while Cardinal Wolsey still ruled England. Before his death in 1554, he had twice been Mayor of Plymouth and MP for the borough; Henry VIII is said to have been much impressed by his 'wisdom, valour, experience and skill in sea causes', and the King was himself something of a naval expert. His eldest son, another William, followed in his footsteps, owning privateers, investing in voyages and interesting himself in local affairs, though he was to be overshadowed by his younger brother, John Hawkins, born in 1532. During 1559 John had married the daughter of Benjamin Gonson who was, like his father, Treasurer of the Navy, and this connection was to bring him in close contact with the Queen's Court and with officials of the Navy Board, such as Admiral Sir William Wynter. John Hawkins's ventures were to be financed in part by courtiers looking for a sound investment and were to be undertaken largely with royal support. Drake in turn was to build on these foundations, and the close connection between privateering and the navy which the elder man developed was to be extended by the

PREVIOUS PAGES A map of America from Ptolemaeus's *Geographia universalis*, published in Basel in 1545.

OPPOSITE Elizabeth, seen here in an engraving by Chrispin van Queboorn.

A portrait of Elizabeth in a Plea Roll of the Court of Queen's Bench.

younger. Hawkins was destined to follow his father-in-law as Treasurer of the Navy. A William Hawkins of the next generation would sail with Drake on his voyage around the world.

By the time Francis had reached Plymouth, it is probable that John Hawkins had already sailed on his second expedition, for he left the Sound on 18 October 1564. This voyage was on a much more extensive scale, and the Queen and Lord Robert Dudley were among those who had a financial interest in it. Off the West African coast, Hawkins seized various vessels with slaves, ivory and gold and to the protesting Portuguese captains he bombastically replied that the contract for supplying slaves to the New World 'belonged neither to the King of Portugal, nor to the contractors, but to the realm of England and John Hawkins'. To the Spaniards in the Caribbean he made claims in a similarly high tone – that he sailed in those waters 'by order of Elizabeth, Queen of England, whose fleet this is'. He had to fight his way to trade at Borburata in Venezuela and Rio de la Hacha. After his return, the complaints of the Spanish ambassador, de Silva, led the Privy Council to require Hawkins to enter bonds, with heavy penalties, that he would not return to the West Indies, though this deed was entered with a nod and accepted with a wink. Meanwhile, Francis Drake was having his first taste of a voyage beyond the Line.

Privateering in the New World was the child of Spanish colonization. Spain had reserved to herself an entire continent and attempted from the outset to prohibit other nations from trading there; 'all were reported pirates that were found in those waters'. In 1493, two months after Christopher Columbus had returned to Lisbon from his first voyage to the West Indies, Pope Alexander VI published his bull dividing the New World between Spain and Portugal. Ferdinand of Aragon, who had financed the venture, was anxious to guard against Portuguese counter-claims to Spanish dominion across the Atlantic and so the same year he persuaded the Pope to issue a revised bull assigning to Spain all territory west and south of a line, drawn north to south, a hundred leagues west of the Azores; a treaty which Ferdinand signed with the King of Portugal a few months later defined their respective areas of influence even more closely. (Effectively Portugal kept to her colony on the River Plate estuary and concentrated her main efforts in the Far East and India.) English maritime enterprise to North America under the Cabots a few years later was not reckoned a technical breach of the papal ruling, since it was so far to the north of 'the Line', though Englishmen's voyages alarmed

West African tribes shown in a contemporary print. Drake would have seized slaves from among them, to take with him to the New World.

the Spaniards, whose maps already showed the entire coast as Spanish. When Philip of Spain became Queen Mary's consort in 1554, he vigorously supported an expedition which English seamen were preparing for a search for the North-West Passage, not fully aware that this conflicted with the bulls of 1493. Soon, however, it became clear that the Spaniards would not tolerate any infringement of their title to exploit the New World continent, and other nations, denied a foothold for colonization, were prepared to fight for the right to trade in those parts, whatever regulations were issued from Madrid. The rich mineral wealth of America, exploited by the Spanish notably at Potosi, Peru and at Zaateca in Mexico, provoked a financial crisis in Europe as the Plate Fleet crossed the ocean with precious metals twice a year. French and English seamen refused to be barred from a share in this immensely valuable traffic and with the final overthrow of papal power in England, the edicts of 1493 were no longer held binding.

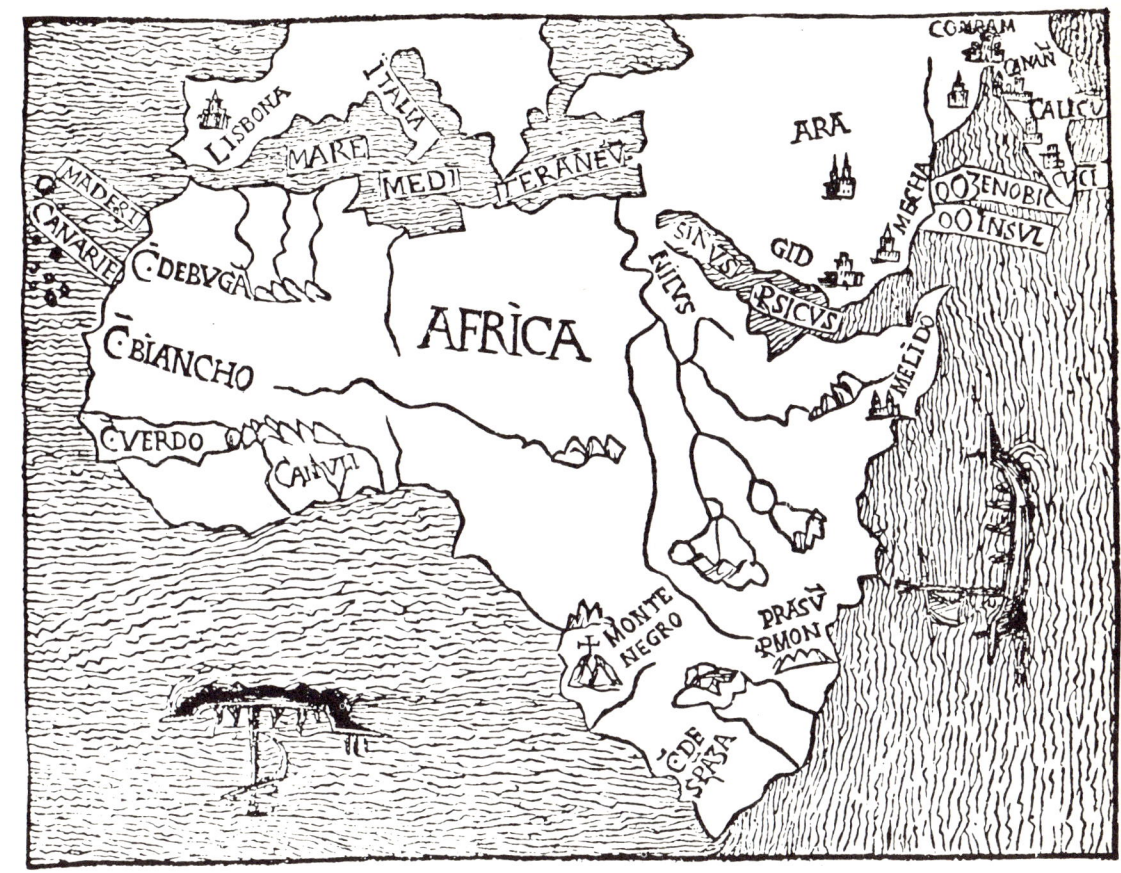

The West African coast – the route which Drake followed, as far south as the Cape Verde Islands and Sierra Leone, before crossing the Atlantic to the Caribbean.

Philip II, so recently Mary's consort, had no wish to cross swords with Englishmen. England was Spain's traditional ally and the commercial relations of England both with Spain and with the Spanish Netherlands were long established and fundamental to the economies of each country. For Philip, France was the traditional enemy, and with his Netherlands provinces impatient of Spanish rule, he wanted at all costs to preserve good relations with Elizabeth; he had hoped in vain to marry her and when she declined his proposal he saw himself as a brotherly protector. And yet Philip could not risk leaving his colonial empire undefended, could not afford to allow the specie from his gold and silver mines to fall into other hands. Up to a point, he would wink at the depredations of English seamen beyond the Line, but there came a time when he could no longer ignore attacks which had important repercussions in Europe. After John Hawkins's first voyage, Philip was determined to see that the Indies were properly

South American natives dancing and preparing food, from Theodore de Bry's book *Americæ Tertia Pars* (1592), which described the voyages of Drake, Magellan and other seafarers of the century.

defended, for he could not tolerate interlopers, let alone freebooters, operating in the Caribbean. During 1565 he commissioned Pero Menéndez de Avilés to destroy the French settlement in Florida, and though a few Frenchmen escaped, Jean Ribault and most of his companions were massacred. In the same year, the King laid down much stricter regulations for the conduct of the two yearly convoys of treasure ships between the Indies and Spain, with a galleon of thirty-six guns as the principal guardship. Menéndez himself was appointed admiral of a squadron of twelve well-armed vessels known as the Galleons of the Indian Guard.

Henceforth the laws against trafficking with interlopers were to be rigorously enforced and those colonial officials who were suspected of turning a blind eye to the rules were replaced. Spanish admirals were even under orders to put interlopers to death, though many escaped immediate execution by being sent before the Inquisition. This tightening of the screw augured ill for John Hawkins and his young cousin, eager to follow in his wake.

Francis Drake left on his first ocean voyage in November 1566 in an expedition for the Hawkins syndicate of four ships which sailed under the command of Captain John Lovell. As in John

Another illustration from de Bry's account: here, the natives are offering fish to European sailors.

A typical sixteenth-century Portuguese ship, showing the observation of the passage of the sun with a portable astrolabe and a cross staff.

Hawkins's recent voyages, they first made for the Guinea Coast in search of the human cargo that they would trade in the Indies. Here they met opposition from the Portuguese and sailed on to the Cape Verde Islands to capture a number of Portuguese craft (in the raid Lovell killed a man). This was Drake's first experience of privateering warfare. Sending one of his ships back to Plymouth with ivory, wax and sugar, Lovell led the rest across the Atlantic with the Negro slaves, expecting a ready sale; indeed, the Spanish at Rio de la Hacha and elsewhere had the slaves on order from Hawkins. It proved a bad moment for Lovell to open for business, for a new governor of Venezuela, under instructions to purge local colonial administration of irregular trafficking with interlopers, was already causing no little embarrassment to Miguel de Castellanos, the Treasurer of Rio, by his strict and detailed enquiries. Castellanos refused to give Lovell licence to trade and made plain that he would oppose by force any attempt to land the ninety Negroes who had survived the Atlantic crossing. Eventually the English captain was forced to let the Spaniards of Rio de la Hacha have the slaves for nothing, as he could not feed them indefinitely. As a slaving voyage this was a disaster and Hawkins later lamented 'the simpleness of my deputies, who knew not how to handle these matters'. He never employed Captain Lovell again. Drake, or Hawkins, would certainly have provoked a show-down with the Treasurer of Rio de la Hacha by using strong-arm methods. For Drake the experience was seminal for learning not merely about Atlantic currents and deep-sea navigation but also about Spanish 'perfidy', as he reckoned it. He never forgot Lovell's misfortune and many years later spoke movingly of 'the wrongs received at Rio Hacha with Captain John Lovell'. In their official report of the affair to Philip II, the people of Rio made much of their exposure to 'notorious danger' and the glory they had earned for compelling 'so many valorous enemies to retire' – largely because they hoped to be awarded the proceeds of the sale of the abandoned Negroes. For Francis Drake, the incident underlined the fact that the days of peaceful commerce with the Spanish New World had passed. One other feature of the voyage which he never forgot was his successful conversion of a Welsh seaman of Roman Catholic tendencies to the Protestant faith. When he returned with Lovell to Plymouth in August 1567, he found that his old father, stout Protestant to the end, had died at Upchurch. It was perhaps at this time that his younger brothers John, Joseph and Thomas came to join him at Plymouth.

Drake felt that he had graduated in a new branch of seamanship – the world of long voyages, Atlantic rollers, trade winds and tropical storms, of living with problems of fresh-water supplies and careening hulls, and jogging along for months on end with the same shipmates at close quarters. Such was an entirely different mode of life from serving on a coaster in the English Channel, rarely out of sight of his native shore. The voyage with Lovell had given him a taste for adventure as a privateer, and the fact that the enemy who deemed all Englishmen operating in the

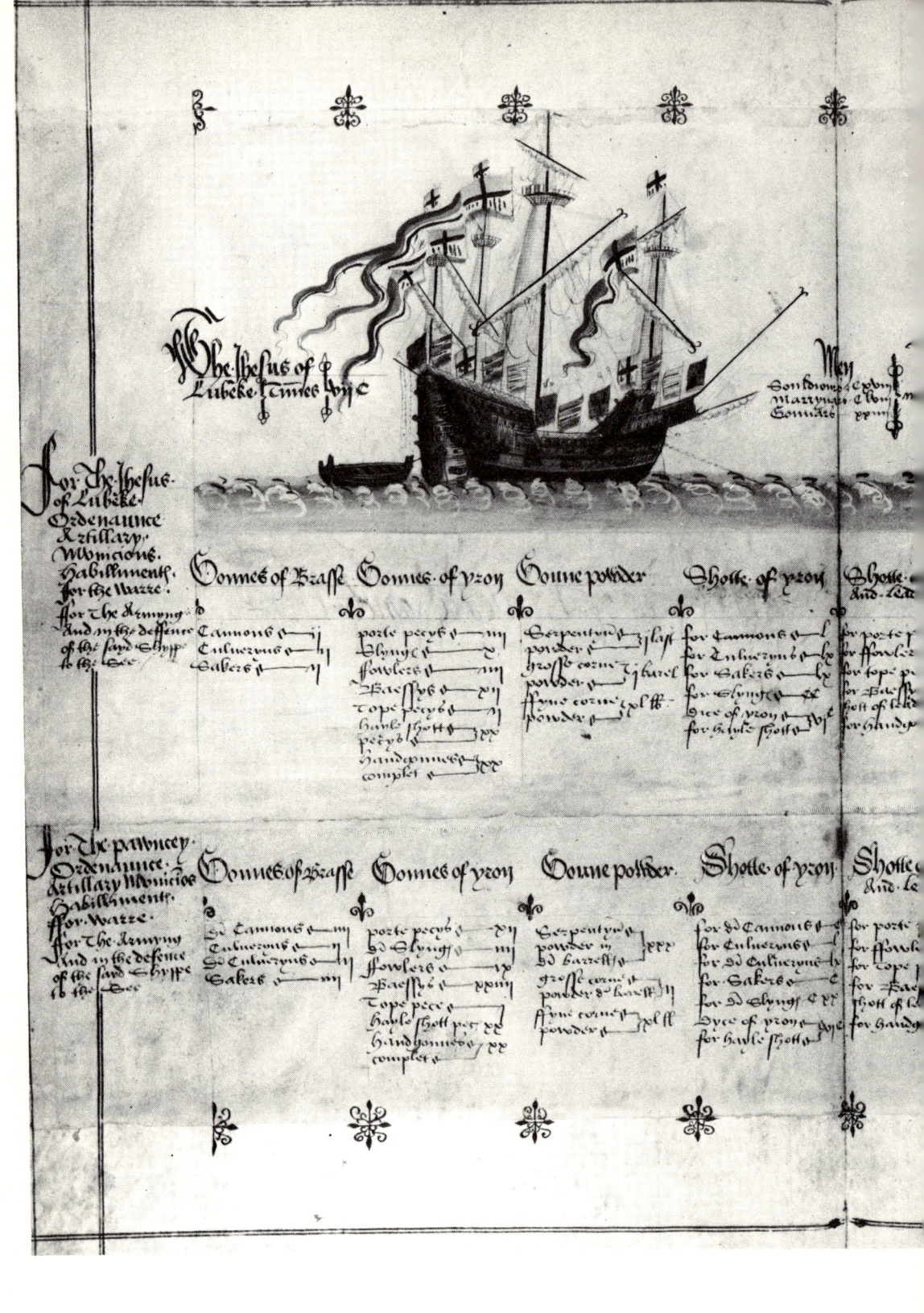

The Jhesus of Lubeke tunes vijᶜ

Men
Sondiours — lxxx
Marrynars — clxx
Gonners — xxx

For the Jhesus of Lubeke Ordenaunce Artillary Mvnicions habillments for the Warre.

for the kepyng and in the deffence of the sayd Shypp to the See

Gonnes of Brass	Gonnes of yron	Goune powder	Shotte of yron	Shotte and Lead
Cannons — ij	porte peces — iiij	Serpentyne powder — ij last	for Cannons — l	for porte p
Culuerens — iij	Slynges — iiij	Crosse corne powder — ij barel	for Culuerens — lx	for ffowler
Sakers — ij	ffowlers — iiij	ffyne corne powder — xl ℔	for Sakers — lx	for tope p
	Basses — xij		for Slynges — xx	for Basses
	Tope peces — ij		Dice of yron — xlvj	shott of Lead
	Hayle shott peces — xx		for hayle shott — xbj	for handg
	Handgonnes complet — xxx			

For the pawncey Ordenaunce Artillary Munycions habillments for Warre. for the kepyng and in the defence of the sayd Shypp to the See

Gonnes of Brass	Gonnes of yron	Goune powder	Shotte of yron	Shotte and Le
Cannons — iij	porte peces — vj	Serpentyne powder in bj barrells	for sd Cannons — l	for porte
Culuerens — iij	Slynges — iiij	grosse corne powder — j barel	for Culuerens — lx	for ffowler
sd Culueryns — iij	ffowlers — iiij	ffyne corne powder — xl ℔	for sd Culuerens — lx	for tope
Sakers — iij	Basses — xviij		for Sakers — c	for Bass
	Tope peces		for sd Slynges — xx	shott of Lead
	Hayle shott per — xx		Dice of yron — lxvj	for handg
	Handgonnes complet — xx		for Hayle shott	

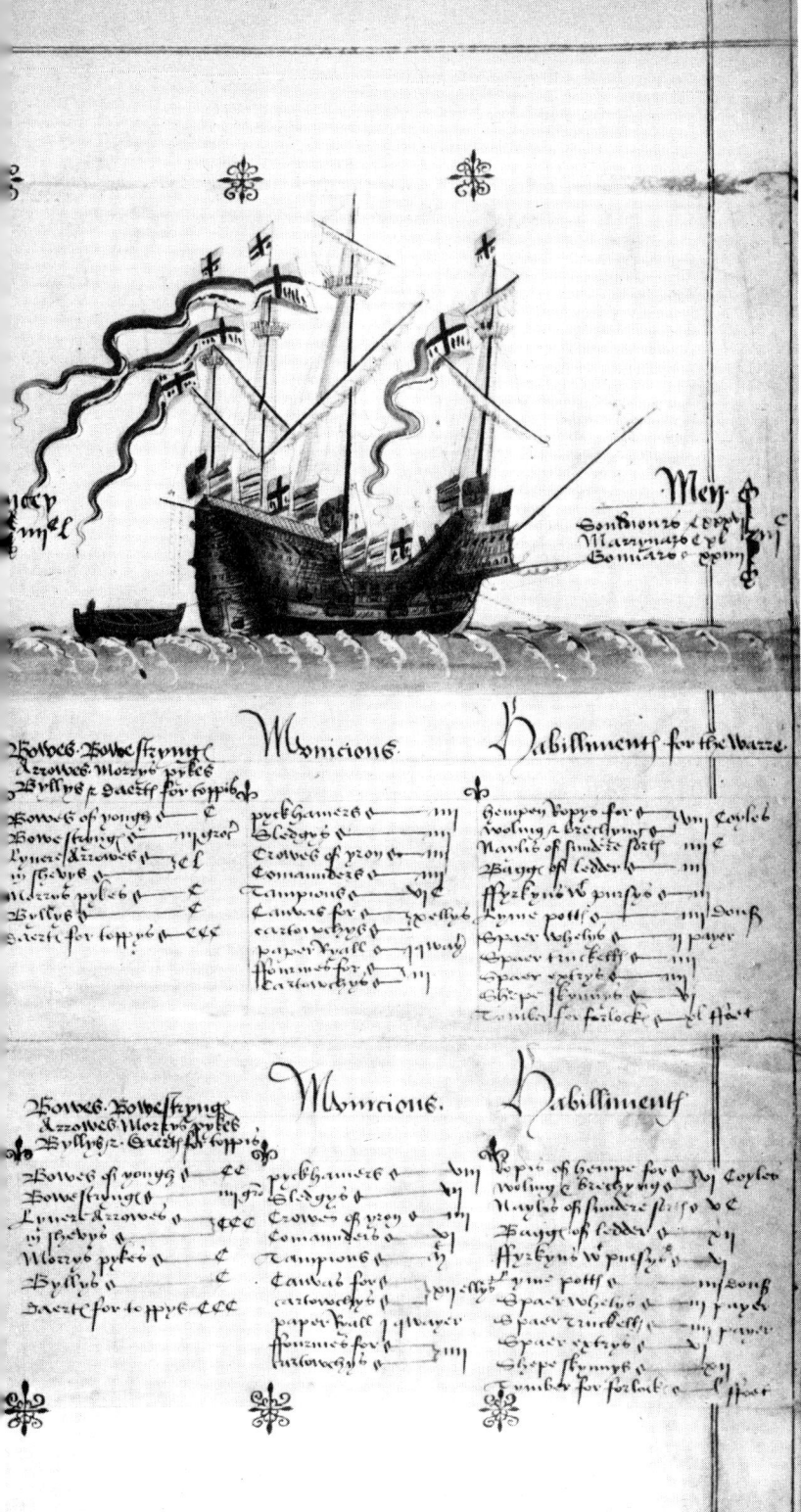

English ships of the kind that Drake was used to – pages from a manuscript which both illustrates them and specifies their munitions. The ship on the left is the *Jesus of Lübeck*.

West Indies as interlopers was a Catholic power made him the readier to fight. While he was away, Hawkins had been preparing for a further expedition, in spite of his bond not to sail west, and was being assigned two of the Queen's ships for it – the old *Jesus of Lübeck* and the *Minion* – to join four of his own vessels. While Lovell had disgraced himself, John Hawkins must have been satisfied with Francis's performance on that voyage, for he found room for him in his new enterprise and before the fleet had left the Cape Verde Islands was to place him in command of the *Judith*. Drake had not been ashore more than six weeks before he was off again.

Before the fleet sailed, however, there was a remarkable incident in Plymouth Sound, when a squadron from the Spanish Netherlands under Baron de Wachen came into port with its flags close-hauled. Hawkins felt it a gross insult that the Flemish Admiral had not dipped his flags; moreover, he did not like the fact that the ships were sailing in the direction of his own isolated anchorage at Catwater, as if intending to run down the *Jesus of Lübeck*, in which Drake was serving, and his other vessels. But a few warning shots sufficed to make the Admiral alter course and to make the customary salute. Hawkins was later taken to task by Queen and Council for risking an incident which might have had most serious consequences; but he defended himself: 'I had rather Her Highness found fault with me for keeping her ships and people to her honour, than to lose them for the glory of others.'

The 'glory' of the *Jesus of Lübeck*, however, belonged to a past age and in a gale that blew up off Brest she began to leak badly and remained a liability for months to come. After a *rendez-vous* in the Canaries, the six vessels made for the West African coast. Here, in the estuaries between Cape Verde and Sierra Leone, they found little chance of trading for slaves, but had to run the gauntlet of the Portuguese. In the hopes of being rewarded with slaves, Hawkins led his men ashore to help a native chief sack a town belonging to a neighbouring chieftain. In these waters he seized a Portuguese caravel that was sailing under a French privateer, named Bland, whom he forced to join the expedition for the Indies, and the fact that there were now seven ships led to Drake's being given a command, first in the privateer and later in the *Judith*, a ship of fifty tons. One vessel, the tiny *William and John*, foundered with all hands lost, but the others reached Dominica in the Lesser Antilles after fifty-two days, at the end of March 1568, and from there they sailed on to Margarita, a small island off Venezuela, to obtain fresh provisions. Here the English Captain introduced himself by formal letter to the governor:

Worshipful, I have touched in your island only to the intent of to refresh my men with fresh victuals, which from my money or wares you shall sell me, meaning to stay only about five or six days here at the furthest. In which time you may assure yourself, and so all others, that by me or any of mine there shall no damage be done to any man; the which also the Queen's Majesty of England, my mistress, at my departure out of England commanded me to have great care of and to serve with my Navy the King of Spain, my old master, if in places where I came any of his stood in need,

John Hawkins

At Borburata on the mainland of Venezuela, there was a blank refusal when the English sought permission to trade, yet they stayed there for eight weeks and, in the teeth of official prohibition, contrived to do a brisk trade, even in slaves. Drake was sent on in advance with the *Judith* and the *Angel* to open negotiations for trading at Rio de la Hacha, where Lovell had been so unlucky – and so timid – the year before. Hawkins deliberately chose Francis for this task. There was no question of Drake's meekly requesting permission from Miguel de Castellanos, the King's Treasurer at Rio, so from the anchorage his guns sent a couple of shots through the Treasurer's house. Judging by the fire from the shore batteries, the port was heavily defended; he moved his ships out of range to anchor until the *Jesus of Lübeck* and the other craft arrived in another five days. Drake told Hawkins that the men of Rio de la Hacha were quite prepared to fight and hoped that his commander would decide on a swift, forceful action, but Hawkins diplomatically sent the Treasurer a letter rehearsing past dealings, including Lovell's abortive visit, and made quite clear that he had a good consignment of slaves for sale, so he hoped that his inherent right to trade would not be denied him. If, in the morning, he added, the Treasurer should see armed men ashore, 'let it nothing trouble you, for as you shall command they shall return aboard again. Showing me this pleasure, you shall command anything I have.' The message was obvious. When next day Hawkins landed three hundred men some two miles from the port and led them into battle, the Spaniards and their Negro allies failed to show the spirit that Castellanos himself displayed; they fled from the place, leaving Hawkins master of the town.

The Treasurer remained adamant about trading. Even if the town were in enemy hands, he would not allow them to barter.

Some houses were fired and then one of the Treasurer's own slaves came into town and agreed to show the English where all the valuables had been hidden. The rest of the Spaniards now rose against Castellanos to force him to come to terms with the invaders. He at last accepted the situation and (perhaps with a view to having his words reported in Madrid, where the authorities might realize the full difficulty of his position) said to his fellow sufferers: 'There is not one of you that knoweth John Hawkins. He is such a man that any man talking with him hath no power to deny him anything he doth request.' Soon there was brisk trading, after Hawkins had given sixty slaves as compensation for burning various buildings, though he did extract a sizeable ransom for sparing the church.

Next they proceeded to Santa Marta, where after secret conversations with a governor of a very different stamp from Castellanos, a military landing was staged in full battle array, with guns from the ships blazing away. The town surrendered in a matter of minutes and no one on either side suffered a scratch. At least the governor hoped that he had saved his credit with his colonial fellows and his reputation with the government at home. Cartagena was too tough a nut to crack, but the English stayed on an island in the bay, used as a holiday resort by the wealthier Spaniards, and found a store of wine, which Hawkins seized, leaving in its place various English wares. Although he had not sold all his slaves, he was running short of provisions and decided to make for home *via* the western Caribbean and the Florida Channel, but off Cuba the fleet met with a heavy gale in which the *Jesus of Lübeck* almost foundered. Hawkins could not find a suitable harbour in Florida in which he could have running repairs made, and after a further storm in the Gulf of Florida, of which he had no reliable charts, he came across a Spanish vessel whose commander advised him to make for San Juan de Ulua – the only port, he said, which was both safe and suitable. This was the harbour from which the specie from the Mexican silver mines was shipped to Spain; it was in fact the port for Vera Cruz, which lay fifteen miles to the north.

The Plate Fleet was daily expected at San Juan de Ulua and when Hawkins arrived, the Spanish thought that his flotilla were the ships from Spain, so he received a warm welcome. Thanks to this confusion, he had gained a peaceful entry to the harbour, but he could not reckon how long his luck would last. The officials granted his request for provisions and facilities to repair the *Jesus*

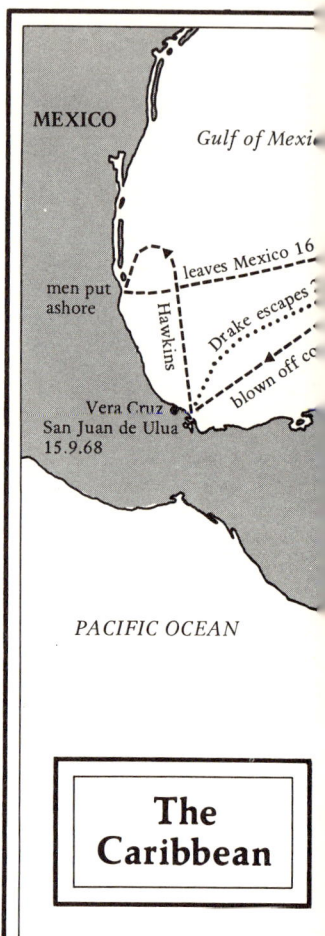

The Caribbean

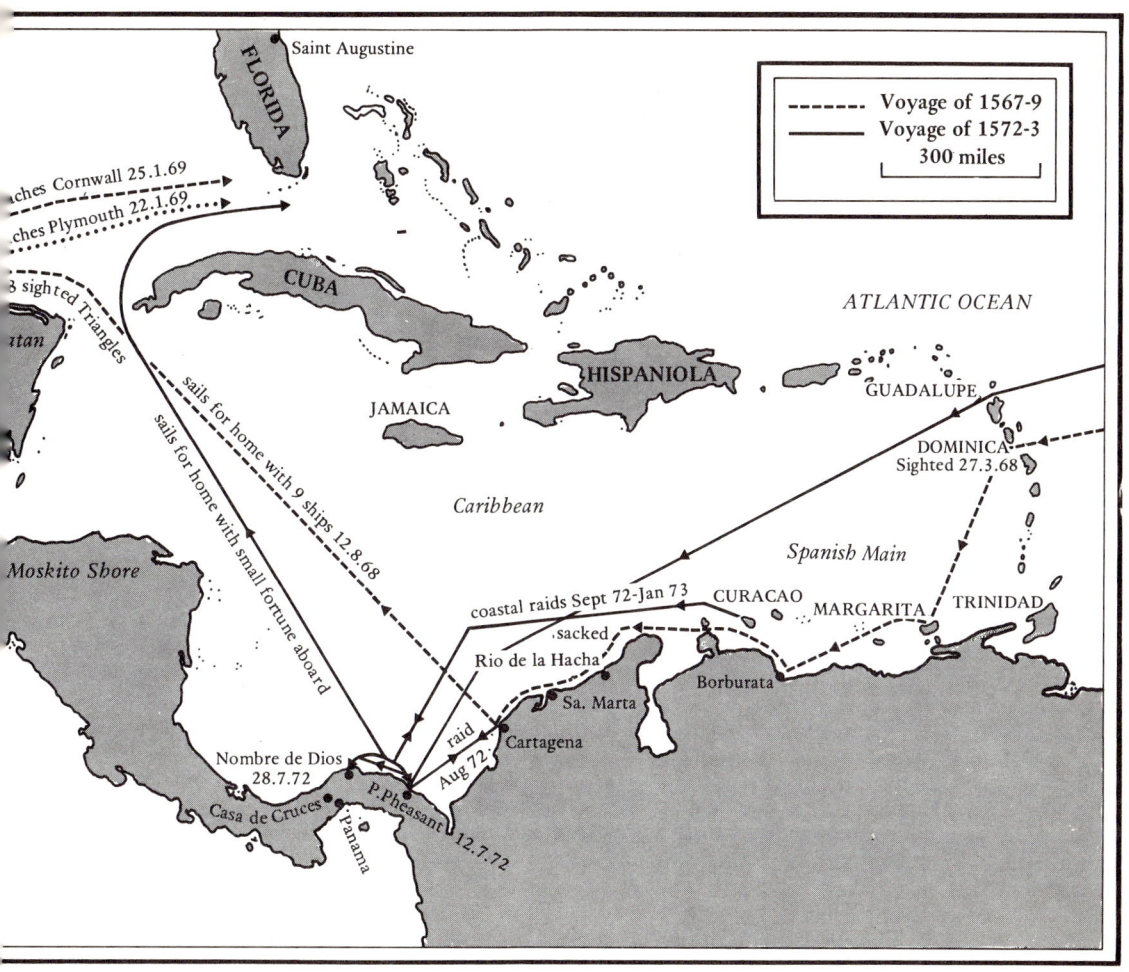

of *Lübeck*. Two days later, the Plate Fleet, all thirteen sail, came into view. At this critical moment, Hawkins took charge of the shore batteries, at first intending to prevent the Spanish fleet from entering until he was himself ready to leave. But he soon learned that the fleet had aboard the new Viceroy of Mexico, Don Martin Enriquez, and it would have been most irregular for the English commander to have denied him access. There were Spanish cries of 'The Lutherans are upon us.' Hawkins then sought assurances from the Spanish that if he allowed the well-armed Plate Fleet to enter harbour, he and his compatriots would not suffer. As a result, hostages were exchanged and Hawkins's right to victual and refit his vessels was confirmed. Little did he suspect that the hostages sent to him were all men of straw, and he took at its face

47

Navigation in the Sixteenth Century

The instruments of navigation which Drake would have used may seem rudimentary to us now, but they represented a great advance on those of his predecessors. The Englishman was evidently ahead of his Spanish rivals in the field of cartography, for the charts and pictorial records which he and his nephew kept of the voyages both impressed and alarmed the captive Don Francisco de Zarate with their accuracy.

ABOVE A compass design from a Spanish map of 1582 by Juan Martinez de Recalde.

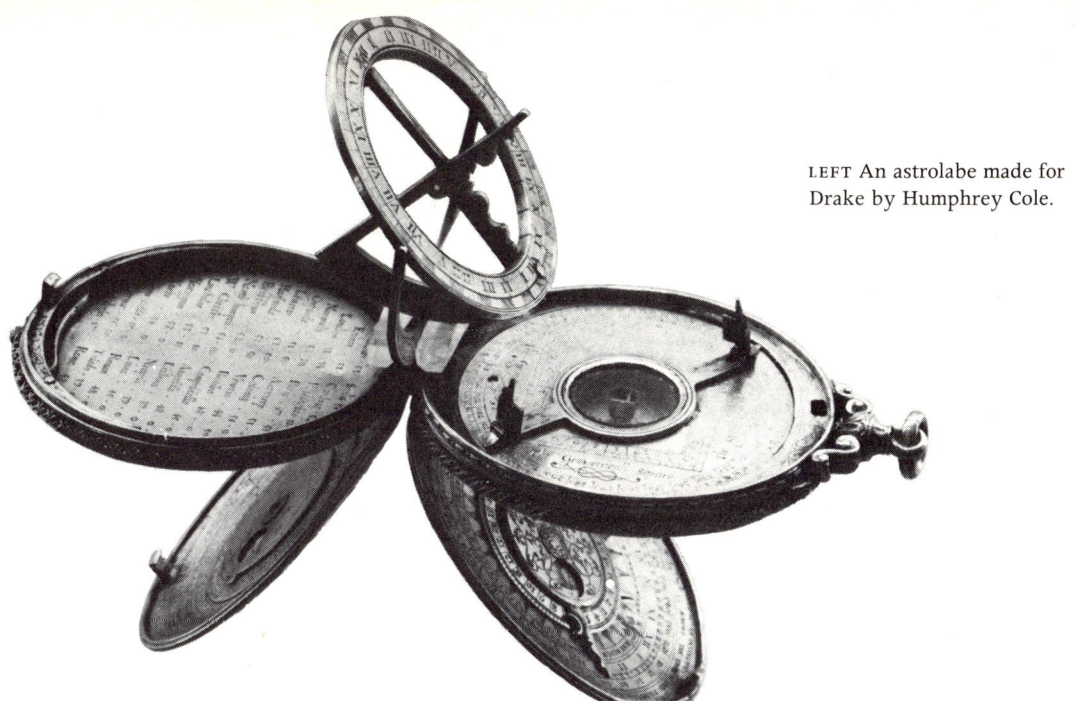

LEFT An astrolabe made for Drake by Humphrey Cole.

LEFT *The Navigator* by Stradanus – an engraving showing the whole repertoire of navigational instruments available by the beginning of the seventeenth century.

RIGHT A movable compass for the stars, illustrated with the central portion turned round, in Wagener's *The Mariners Mirrour* of 1586.

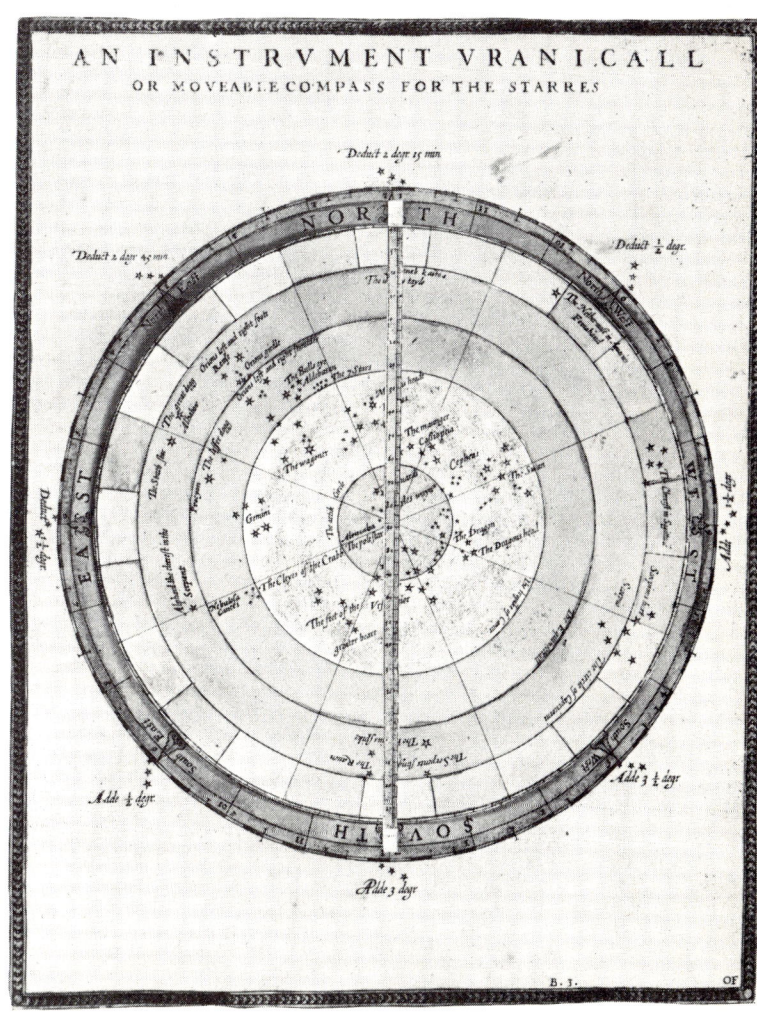

value the Spanish pledge that no soldiers would be landed. Don Martin, however, was in no mood to keep to these terms and at once he sent to Vera Cruz for as strong a force as could be mustered, while he made plans to board the English craft. Hawkins noticed the suspicious movement of ships in the harbour and sent one of his men to lay a formal complaint that the truce was being broken; that man was never seen again. Then the English troops manning the guns on the island were surprised by a strong force from Vera Cruz. Moving his vessel by warping, Hawkins sank by gunfire two Spanish men-of-war, but he could not hope to rig his sails and escape, so he ordered the men and cargo in the *Jesus* to be transferred, partly to the *Judith*, partly to the *Minion*. Before this had been completed, the Spaniards sent down two fireships on the tide and in the ensuing panic the *Jesus of Lübeck* was abandoned. Those of the crew who were lucky enough jumped to safety on the *Minion*, the rest perished. Hawkins lost aboard her his fine set of gold dinner-plate with other effects. Now he had only two ships.

The *Minion* under Hawkins's command and the *Judith* under Drake both moved in the dark well out of range of the Spanish guns. By one account, Hawkins 'then willed Master Drake to come' alongside the *Minion* 'to take in men and other things needful; and so he did'. Later there was misunderstanding between the two, for during the night Drake weighed anchor to start on the long homeward journey; as Hawkins put it, the *Judith* 'forsook us in our great misery'. It seems that Drake had lost contact with his admiral and, believing that the *Minion* had suffered a similar fate to the *Jesus of Lübeck* he decided to save his ship, his men and his cargo by leaving San Juan de Ulua. Years afterwards, William Borough taunted Francis for deserting his compatriots. Certainly Hawkins, in the aftermath of his tribulations on the Mexican coast, felt that his cousin had abandoned him. Yet Drake's character, especially his imperturbable courage, and the whole of his subsequent career make it seem most unlikely that he knowingly left a ship in difficulty to fend against the enemy and the elements unaided. The most reasonable explanation is that, with deteriorating weather and the problems of making his provisions go round the extra men he had already taken aboard, he felt it his duty to make his way home independently, where he arrived on 20 January 1569 with sixty-five men after a far from comfortable passage. This return voyage was his first command and it was no mean feat to have come through the ordeal. He was appalled when late in the spring he learned from John Hawkins of 'all the miseries and troublesome affairs of this sorrowful voyage'. Because of a dire shortage of food and water, a hundred men in the *Minion* pleaded with Hawkins to be put ashore on the Mexican coast; many of them died from sickness, brought on by malnutrition; others suffered at the hands of the Inquisition, and Drake himself kept special remembrance of Robert Barrett who steadfastly refused to recant his Protestantism and was burned alive in the market-place of Seville. The numbers of those aboard the *Minion* gradually dwindled from starvation and exhaustion so that Hawkins landed in England with only fourteen survivors. With hindsight, perhaps we may think that Drake had acted with more circumspection than had the expedition's commander.

For Francis Drake, no less than for John Hawkins, the battle of San Juan de Ulua was a watershed. 'It showed the merchant adventurers that honest and peaceful trade with the Spanish Indies was no longer possible, except illicitly on a small scale.' There were to be no further English slaving voyages to the Guinea Coast for acquiring Negroes to trade with the Spaniards of the West Indies for a great many years to come, since the Spanish had now made it abundantly clear that they would not stoop to trading with interloping heretics, and so Drake embarked on a career as a privateer in the waters of the New World. Denied the chance of peaceful trade, he would plunder. Henceforth there was to be no peace 'beyond the Line' and each year the peace with Spain in Europe was to become more uncertain until, finally, relations deteriorated into open war in 1586. Drake himself never forgot the treacherous conduct of the Spanish Viceroy of Mexico, Don Martin Enriquez. When, on his voyage round the world eleven years later, he took a high-ranking Spanish officer as his prisoner, Drake asked him if by chance he knew Don Martin; hearing that he did, he replied, 'I would rather meet with him than with all the gold and silver in the Indies, that I might show him how to keep the word of a gentleman.'

3
The Treasure House of the World

ON LANDING AT PLYMOUTH, Drake reported to William Hawkins, who wrote off to the Privy Council, asking for a commission of reprisal to avenge the injuries done to his brother at San Juan, and used Francis as his messenger. Drake found everyone in Plymouth and in London, talking about the seizure of three Spanish ships, made not on the Spanish Main, but in Plymouth Sound. These vessels, bringing money from Spain to pay the Duke of Alva's troops in the Netherlands, had taken refuge from a gale in the Channel and had been impounded by the Queen the previous month. The treasure was already safely locked up in the Tower of London. The repercussions of this incident were considerable, for relations with Spain and the Netherlands had been broken off, while protracted negotiations opened on the manner of the restitution of the booty. English merchants were now in the thick of a grave financial crisis and blamed, in particular, Sir William Cecil, the Principal Secretary of State, for lack of judgment in handling the affair. To many, however, what Drake had to say about events at San Juan de Ulua justified the seizure of Alva's treasure ships. Before long, John Hawkins, too, was in the capital to make known his version of the voyage and he must have discussed with his cousin the rights and wrongs of the campaign. Later in the year, Hawkins published a pamphlet recounting the battle of San Juan in which he moderately chided Francis, without in fact naming him – a chance sentence that the *Judith* 'forsook us in our great misery'. But he had seen enough of Drake's ability on the voyage to judge that he was not a man who deserved to have his chosen career terminated by adverse criticism in print, or by snide remarks on the quays of Plymouth, so Hawkins behaved charitably. Drake was in any case a relative and down on his fortunes, for according to one account, he left San Juan de Ulua 'with the loss of all his means'. He was not among those examined in the High Court of Admiralty later in the year.

As likely as not, Francis Drake sailed one of Admiral Wynter's men-of-war that went to escort the convoy of merchantmen carrying English cloth to the Hamburg trade fair. The German port had been chosen as an alternative Continental centre to Antwerp, which was closed to English merchants under the embargo. We know for certain that Drake was in Devon by Midsummer for on 4 July he married Mary Newman at the parish church of St Budeaux, on the Tamar, just north of Plymouth. Francis was by now about twenty-five, his bride perhaps seventeen. Very little is known of Mary, except that she came from a seafaring family,

PREVIOUS PAGES Spanish galleons in the 1550s.

OPPOSITE Lord Burghley, riding his mule in his garden.

RIGHT John Dee, the much admired mathematician, astrologer and geographer. In 1564 he was appointed royal adviser in mystic secrets, including alchemy.

OPPOSITE The title page to Dee's treatise on the *Art of Navigation*

for her father, Harry Newman, had sailed with Hawkins in the *Jesus of Lübeck*. Harry shared Francis's militant religious outlook, for he had the reputation of being 'a great Lutheran' who inveighed 'against the Roman Church and argued for Protestant doctrines'. If Mary had been swept off her feet by a man already highly regarded in Plymouth for his prowess at sea, she at least entered marriage with her eyes open. Mariners' wives, as her mother had always warned her, were condemned to painful 'farewells', long separations and constant anxieties about the safety of their menfolk. News and even informed rumour was hard to come by when ships had sailed for the Spanish Main, and the women would go down to Mill Bay to pick up such crumbs for their comfort as they could gather. Mary Drake was to suffer more

Breaming a ship: a detail from a woodcut in Bernhard von Breydenbach's *Peregrinationes in Terram Sanctam,* published in Mainz in 1486.

than most, for she had no child to lavish her affections upon and distract her from her perennial worries about Francis.

The year 1570 saw him in the Caribbean, having the command of two small vessels, the *Swan* and the *Dragon*, on a trading voyage in which Sir William Wynter was the principal shareholder. It was a peaceful expedition that has left no mark on history, yet Drake's experience on it led him to return the next year in the *Swan* on his own account, putting into the voyage the proceeds of his last venture. He wanted to operate independently so that he could reconnoitre the waters of the Panama Isthmus, learn all he could about the land route by which the Peruvian treasure, landed at Panama on the Pacific, was brought by mule-train across the Isthmus and taken to the Caribbean port of Nombre de Dios, and if possible make contact with the Cimaroons, to enlist their aid for future operations against the Spanish. Drake would snap up any prizes that came his way, but his main objective was to plan for the future by observing, prospecting and searching for a secret haven, which might become his private base in the heart of the Spanish dominions of central America. No corsair had planned operations with such infinite care, but the ultimate prize he sought was nothing less than a key to the 'Treasure House of the World'. The produce of the American gold and silver mines, stored at Nombre de Dios ready for transportation to Spain, could come into his hands if things went well, and be landed at Plymouth.

If no other Englishman had the boldness to plan on such a scale, there was, he soon discovered, a Frenchman who had been almost as strikingly hypnotized by the glint of Spanish gold. This was Nicholas des Isles (though he had several *aliases*), who had been exploring the Chagres River that flows into the Caribbean just north of Panama. Des Isles had taken a runaway slave from Nombre de Dios, from whom he gleaned information about the Cimaroon people dwelling in the jungles of the Isthmus. These were Negro slaves who had escaped from their masters and formed independent communities which the Spaniards could never subdue. The Bishop of Panama reckoned that of the thousand Negroes who were transported to the Main each year from West Africa, over three hundred succeeded in escaping to the wilds. Drake talked over his own scheme with des Isles and together they mapped out a plan to use Cimaroon warriors as allies in attacking the Spanish mule-trains laden with treasure bound for Nombre de Dios and in waylaying the small craft with less valuable commodities that used the Chagres River. Theirs was to be a commando raid undertaken with as much detailed local knowledge as possible, otherwise it would have no chance of success. The Englishman learned much about the Spanish settlements and the state of their defences and he was satisfied that Nombre de Dios was inadequately protected. No less important, he surveyed creeks and waterways from his pinnace, familiarizing himself with shoaling and other hazards, sketching the appearance of the coast and even visiting Nombre de Dios, disguised as a Spaniard, to gain first-hand knowledge of the harbour and the plan of the town.

Drake: his early experiences in the Caribbean prepared him for the incredible feat of his circumnavigation of the world.

Finally he had discovered an ideal lair, which he named 'Port Pheasant' after the plentiful game and fish which he found there. He described it as 'a fine round bay of very safe harbour for all winds, lying between two high points, no part half-a-cable length over at the mouth, but within eight or ten cables every way, having ten or twelve fathom water, more or less, full of good fish, the soil also very fruitful'. The exact location of this demi-paradise, on the Acla coast, on the western side of the Gulf of Darien, has never been determined, for Drake understandably kept his secret, but the most likely candidate is Puerto Escoces. To this landlocked harbour he brought various prizes he had captured, buried his surplus stores and, bidding *adieu* to des Isles, made for home, confident that he was well poised for inflicting a terrible wound on Spain which would bring him fame and riches.

Since commercial relations between England and Spain were still severed, Drake saw no difficulties in obtaining authority and finance for his expedition. The moment was ripe for action, for the Spanish ambassador, Gerau de Spes, had been expelled from England for his share in the Ridolfi Plot to assassinate Queen Elizabeth and liberate Mary, Queen of Scots (a prisoner in England since the time Drake was at San Juan de Ulua). Moreover, in the late autumn came news of a decisive Spanish naval victory, when Don John of Austria annihilated the Turkish fleet at the battle of Lepanto. In Europe, Spain seemed invincible, but in the Americas, Drake was sure she was vulnerable. On the day on which he sailed west in May 1572, Lewis of Nassau seized Mons in the Netherlands and prepared to withstand the Spanish Duke of Alva.

Francis Drake had only two ships for his enterprise, his flagship, the *Pasco* (or *Pasche*) of seventy tons belonging to John Hawkins, and his own ship, the *Swan*, less than half that size, which was commanded by his brother, John Drake; in the total company of seventy-three was another brother, Joseph. A heaven-sent wind sped them across the Atlantic to reach the Caribbean in a mere thirty-five days. After watering at Guadalupe, they made straight for the secret haven of 'Port Pheasant'. Drake was alarmed to find that the stores he had hidden the previous summer had been rifled and when he went ashore to investigate a tell-tale wisp of smoke, he discovered a message from John Garrett, a Plymouth captain, written only five days before: 'Captain Drake, if you fortune to come to this port make haste away, for the [slaves of the] Spaniards which you had with you here last year have betrayed the place and taken away all that you left here.' Garrett, expecting

Drake to return, had nailed his letter to a tree and lit a fire nearby, now in its last embers, to attract attention. It was a severe blow that the Spaniards had discovered his hide-out, but at least they had no idea exactly when he would be returning. Instead of being scared off, he built a stockade and had his men assemble the pinnaces which he had brought from Plymouth in sections for using in the shallows where not even the *Swan* could sail. Next day there arrived in the harbour a privateering bark belonging to Sir Edward Horsey, the captain of the Isle of Wight, which was commanded by James Ranse, and he had with him two prizes he had taken. Drake assumed that one of the *Swan*'s crew had blabbed in Plymouth about 'Port Pheasant' the previous summer and now, to make the best of an awkward situation, he persuaded Ranse to join forces with him in his projected attack on Nombre de Dios. At the Isle of Pines, Drake met with two frigates manned by Negro slaves who were taking aboard timber. He questioned them closely to find out the latest news from Nombre de Dios and then set them free ashore to join the Cimaroons, making it plain that no one must reveal to the Spanish his presence in those waters – as his account of the voyage pithily puts it, 'he was loath to put the town to too much expense, which he knew they would willingly bestow, in providing beforehand for his entertainment!'

The little fleet continued up the coast and came to anchor at night in a secluded bay, behind a promontory to the east of Nombre de Dios harbour. Ranse and his crew were left to guard the ships while Drake and his company set off in the pinnaces by moonlight in the small hours of 28 July. Stealthily they came ashore at about 3 a.m. while the town slept. Some of the men thought it a foolhardy enterprise, but Drake spurred them on to what he said would be a famous victory. From his topographical knowledge, he seemed to know the darkened town as well as he did the streets of Plymouth; he knew exactly where the shore battery was, with a lone gunner in charge, and the man and his six cannons were silenced. To create a diversion, John Drake and John Oxenham were sent off with a party to attack the town from the west side, and having placed twelve men to guard the pinnaces, Francis led his main force to a hill on the east, from which he would march on the King's Treasure House down by the waterside.

There was soon panic in Nombre de Dios. Bells were rung to alarm the townsfolk still abed and the Spaniards were deceived by the division of the English into two bands into thinking them a much more powerful force than they were. As Drake brought his men to the market-place, however, with drums beating and trumpets sounding, enough soldiers had mustered to bar his approach to the Panama Gate. In a sharp clash, an English trumpeter fell and Drake himself was wounded by a shot in the thigh, though he concealed his pain, and the enemy were answered by fierce musket fire and some well-directed arrows. They took to their heels when John Drake's small party entered the fray, shouting the traditional war cry 'St George'. Two prisoners were forced to lead the Englishmen to the Governor's House, which they forced open to find an enormous quantity of silver in heavy bars. Drake decided that valuable though this was, it was too heavy a prize to be burdened with, while there was still strong hope of a hoard of gold; he forbade his men to touch the silver, for if they could force the doors of the King's Treasure House they would find more gold than their pinnaces could possibly carry. At this juncture, a messenger from the boats on the shore warned Drake that he must be clear of the town by dawn for they understood that reinforcements were on the way. As luck would have it, before they could force the Treasure House, there was a tropical thunderstorm which not only wasted a valuable half-hour but soaked much of their powder and match and damaged their bow strings. Despondency set in, but Drake had never had room for craven cowards, and would not tolerate waiverers at such a time and in such a place. 'I have brought you to the treasure-house of the world', he barked at them. 'If you leave without it you may henceforth blame nobody but yourselves.' Oxenham and young Drake were soon forcing their way into the building, while their captain said that he would see that the market place was held.

Then there were two simultaneous disasters: it was found that the Treasure House was quite empty and Drake collapsed from loss of blood. Despite his careful plans and enquiries, he had not known that for greater security treasure was now sent from Panama only when the vessels forming the Plate Fleet had anchored at Nombre de Dios and as the last fleet had left for Spain a mere six weeks earlier, the Treasure House would remain empty for many months. Drake's collapse was no less unnerving, especially since not a man was aware of his injury; now his wound was known, people belatedly observed that his blood had been filling the prints of his footsteps for some time and they 'thought it not credible that one man should be able to spare so much blood and live'. Thoroughly disheartened, the Englishmen carried Drake

A detailed map of Central and South America, taken from de Bry's *Americæ Tertia Pars* and showing most of the places Drake visited.

to the pinnaces, praying that he might live to fight another day.

The attack on Nombre de Dios had failed inasmuch as they returned to the fleet without gold, without silver even (though the more daring had pickings of one kind or another), with a trumpeter dead and their captain injured. Yet their exploit had shown how easily a Spanish stronghold could be surprised and, but for the tropical storm and the chance wounding of their leader, the English would have made a significant haul. As it was, they still managed to seize a wine ship from the Canaries as they left the bay, to make a temporary base on a small island, where Drake rapidly recovered his strength and his spirits. The Governor of Nombre de Dios sent a messenger to him to try to fathom his intentions, under cover of offering food and asking advice on how to treat wounds received from poisoned arrows. Drake replied curtly that he was Francis Drake, an Englishman, and never poisoned his arrowheads – in much the same way as a Montgomery or a Rommel would in his day despise a general who seriously contemplated using poison gas. As to supplies, he said, the English party lacked nothing, apart, that is to say, from that 'special commodity which that country yieldeth' (meaning gold) – and he warned the man to advise his master to keep on the alert because he intended to reap some of the 'harvest which they get out of the earth and send to Spain to trouble all the earth'. Before he left, the messenger was entertained to an English dinner and loaded with presents so that he said that he had never been so much honoured in all his life. After a while, Captain Ranse decided that there was no point in remaining any longer in the Caribbean; he had his own prizes and a share of the ship with the Canary wine, so he made for home, but Drake was determined to wait for the next Plate Fleet. Henceforward he would plan the details of a raid less comprehensively and from experience learn to improvise and make snap decisions. It is clear that detailed planning was a matter which John Hawkins had inculcated in him but from now on Drake was to be very much his own strategist and his methods were ideally suited to the warfare and conditions of the Spanish Main. In a way, he had outstripped his tutor, born into a different world. Drake could not believe that the new type of warfare he represented – making use of soldiers ashore and artillery afloat in combined operations – would not succeed. In Oliver Cromwell's day, admirals, such as Robert Blake, were officially termed 'generals at sea' but their role had been fashioned by Francis Drake's own experience.

The months of waiting in the Spanish Main were filled with exploits to keep up his men's morale. But life was far from easy. Fever was endemic and there was poignancy in the death of Drake's brother Joseph – one of twenty-eight casualties – in January 1573; despite the risk of infection, Francis comforted him in his arms at the end. The little force of seventy-three was becoming seriously depleted and, a heart-rending decision to have to make, Drake came to the conclusion that he must scuttle his *Swan* for lack of men to work her. He ordered the ship's carpenter, Tom Moone, to bore gimlet holes through her bottom at night, though the man pleaded in vain to have the ship saved from this fate. Next day the crew, led by John Drake, who was not in the secret, slaved away at the pumps for hours, but, realizing that she could not be saved, removed everything from her hold and decks before firing the *Swan*.

In surprise raids off Cartagena and Santa Marta, Drake made successful prizes, using his pinnaces in shallow water, and this was still a manner of campaigning that caught the Spanish unawares. Another personal tragedy was the death of his other brother, John, whom Francis had left in command of the *Pasco* while he was exploring the Chagres River. When a Spanish frigate hove in sight, the men were eager to plunder her, but John Drake cautiously advised them that she was probably well armed, whereas the English party were poorly provided with weapons. The others remained anxious to make the attempt, however risky it might prove, and in the end John assented: 'It shall never be said that I will be hindmost, neither shall you report to my brother that you lost your voyage by any cowardice of mine.' As he feared, the frigate was heavily defended and the boarding party he led ran into immediate trouble, having shot discharged in their faces. John was mortally wounded and died within the hour, having dictated a rough will calling on Francis to see that his wife Alice, 'a young woman', was paid the profits of the £30 he had invested in the voyage. It grieved Francis that he was not with him when he died.

Drake spent much of the time searching out the rivers and tracks of the entire Panama Isthmus with the aid of his Cimaroon allies, while others saw to the careening of the ships and putting the pinnaces in first-rate order. With eighteen men, he went with native guides far into the tropical forest. At one point they reached a ridge and here the Negroes said that if Drake climbed a look-out tree on which they had cut notches for footholds, he would be able to see both the 'North Sea' of the Caribbean and the 'great South Sea', or Pacific Ocean. Drake did as he was asked and on that famous day, 11 February 1573, he saw the blue of the Pacific and prayed that 'Almighty God in his goodness would give me life and leave to sail once in an English bottom upon that sea', to which John Oxenham said a heart-felt 'Amen'. Then their trek took them nearer to Panama and they could see the treasure ships arriving from Peru. Soon, when the gold had been checked and packed on mules to follow the lonely path across the Isthmus, Drake would strike.

The Cimaroon scouts at last reported that the caravans were to move off to cross the pampas and Drake waited in the deep undergrowth with his little force, not far from Panama, ready to pounce as soon as they heard the bells on the mules. But the Spaniards sensed that there was danger and were very much on the alert, fearing not so much English hijackers as Cimaroons, who were a far more deadly foe. The first caravan of mules bore not packs of gold but bales of taffeta and silk. Everything went wrong. A seaman who was the worse for liquor ignored Drake's orders and attacked a small convoy of donkeys coming from Venta Cruces bearing nothing of value. The Treasurer of Lima, who was riding along the track with his daughter and his own very valuable belongings, gave the Englishman the slip and warned the treasure-train. The Cimaroons appeared to some as faithless allies, more interested in bloodshed than in booty; and so the great ambush for which Drake had waited for five months ended in a fiasco. For him, however, that glimpse of the Pacific was a marvellous compensation for the treasure that had slipped through his fingers.

The Spaniards now knew that Drake was in the jungle, and, though they could not pin down his exact whereabouts, they were thoroughly alerted. He took his band, augmented by Cimaroons, to attack Venta Cruces on the Sagres River and in the woods outside the township a Spanish captain challenged him. 'What people are you?' 'We are Englishmen.' 'Surrender in the name of King Philip; on the word of a gentleman and a soldier I will use you with all courtesy.' To this Francis replied, 'For the honour of the Queen of England, my mistress, I must pass this way', and he fired at him. His fire was answered by a volley from muskets which mortally wounded John Harris and injured Drake, though not seriously. Venta Cruces was soon his, but it yielded little treasure. The Spaniards were amazed at the benevolent courtesy with which the English treated the women, who had been frightened out of

Callao, the port of Lima, here under attack from the Dutch, in an engraving by Levinius Hulsius.

their wits by the sight of Cimaroon warriors. So the tide had begun to turn in Drake's favour. At about this time also, Drake fell in with a Huguenot privateer, Le Testu from Le Havre, who brought him the news of the Massacre of St Bartholomew's Eve, and his blood boiled at the horrifying details of the persecution of fellow Protestants that were told him. They made a joint operation in the jungle near Nombre de Dios to intercept three caravans of 190 mules, each bearing 300 lbs of silver. They took as much as they could carry and buried the rest.

Another venture was even more profitable. Near the mouth of the Rio Francisco, twenty miles from Nombre de Dios, Drake made a rich haul ashore with the help of his Huguenot and Cimaroon

allies, though Le Testu was wounded in the fray and the English pinnaces were forced to put to sea in heavy weather to escape from a Spanish flotilla. It was a desperate situation, for if the pinnaces were captured or sunk he would be stranded and never reach the *Pasco*. Drake buried the gold plate which they had seized and encouraged his party to construct a raft from young trees brought down by the storm, rigged it with a makeshift sail from a biscuit sack and put to sea accompanied by only one Englishman, two men from Le Testu's crew and a few Cimaroons. The sea was running high and the little craft was often completely submerged during the six hours in which they battled in the blazing heat, with salt and sun blistering their bodies; and yet the men had absolute confidence in him. 'If it pleases God that I should put my foot aboard my frigate', he assured them, 'by one means or another I will get you all aboard too, in spite of all the Spaniards in the Indies.' At last they were sighted by the pinnaces, but their rescuers, while amazed at their courage, grieved when they saw how few Englishmen were on the raft. Drake cheered them by pulling from under his shirt a specimen of the most recent booty – a plate of gold – declaring 'Thank God our voyage is made.' That same night they went back in the pinnaces to rescue the wounded Le Testu and the Englishmen who had remained with him and retrieved the treasure they had buried. Soon they were sharing out the spoils with the Frenchmen, vowing to meet again. Drake decided that the *Pasco* was by now too damaged and leaking to withstand an Atlantic crossing, so he captured a Spanish frigate and transferred his flag to her. Before leaving the Caribbean, he broke up the pinnaces and presented his Cimaroon friends with all the spare ironwork to use for their arrow-heads. With typical bravado, he passed close to Cartagena and then by the Florida passage found the Gulf Stream to bring him home.

It was 9 April 1573, a Sunday, when the strange vessel entered Plymouth Sound. A man on the Hoe recognized Drake's personal ensign as the frigate dropped anchor, and answering the Captain's wave darted off to the parish church to interrupt the sermon with the news that after fifteen months at sea, Drake was home, and (we are told) 'few or none remained with the preacher'. He was eager to report to John Hawkins his success in bringing home perhaps £30,000 in booty, and to tell all England of the terror which he had struck at Nombre de Dios and along the coast. For Drake this remarkable voyage was, he felt, only a beginning. From 'Port Pheasant' or a similar isolated haven, he could repeat

OPPOSITE Walter, Earl of Essex, Lord Deputy of Ireland, into whose service Drake entered on his return from the Caribbean.

Drake in Ireland

Drake returned to England to find that Ireland was in a state of insubordination to the English and torn by civil strife – one of the major problems of domestic policy which faced Elizabeth throughout her long reign. Drake accordingly enlisted to serve the Protestant cause – both on land and at sea – against the troops of foreign Catholic mercenaries supporting the rebels.

Plates from a manuscript illustrating incidents in the Irish conflict. RIGHT A Catholic friar absolves a thief, exhorting him to action against the Protestant 'princes' friends'. However, the penitent meets a gruesome end. FAR RIGHT More bloodshed, and the Queen's loyal soldiers bear away the thief's head.

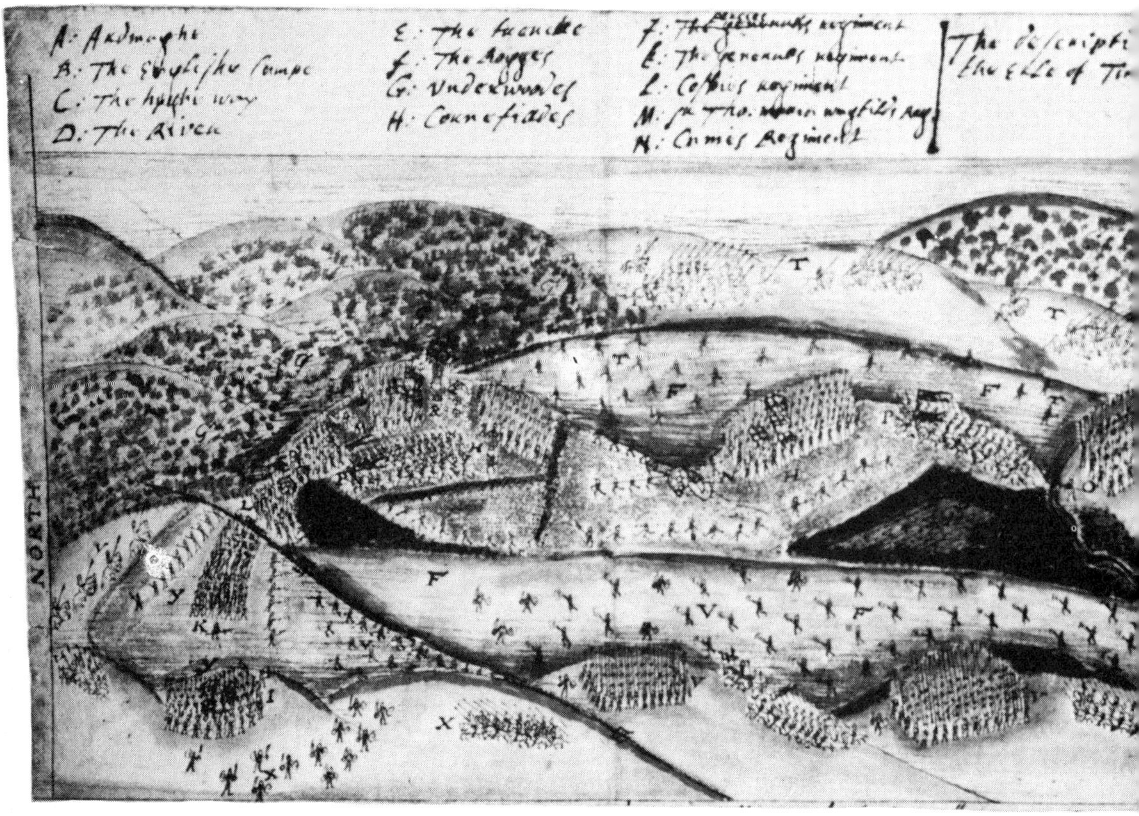

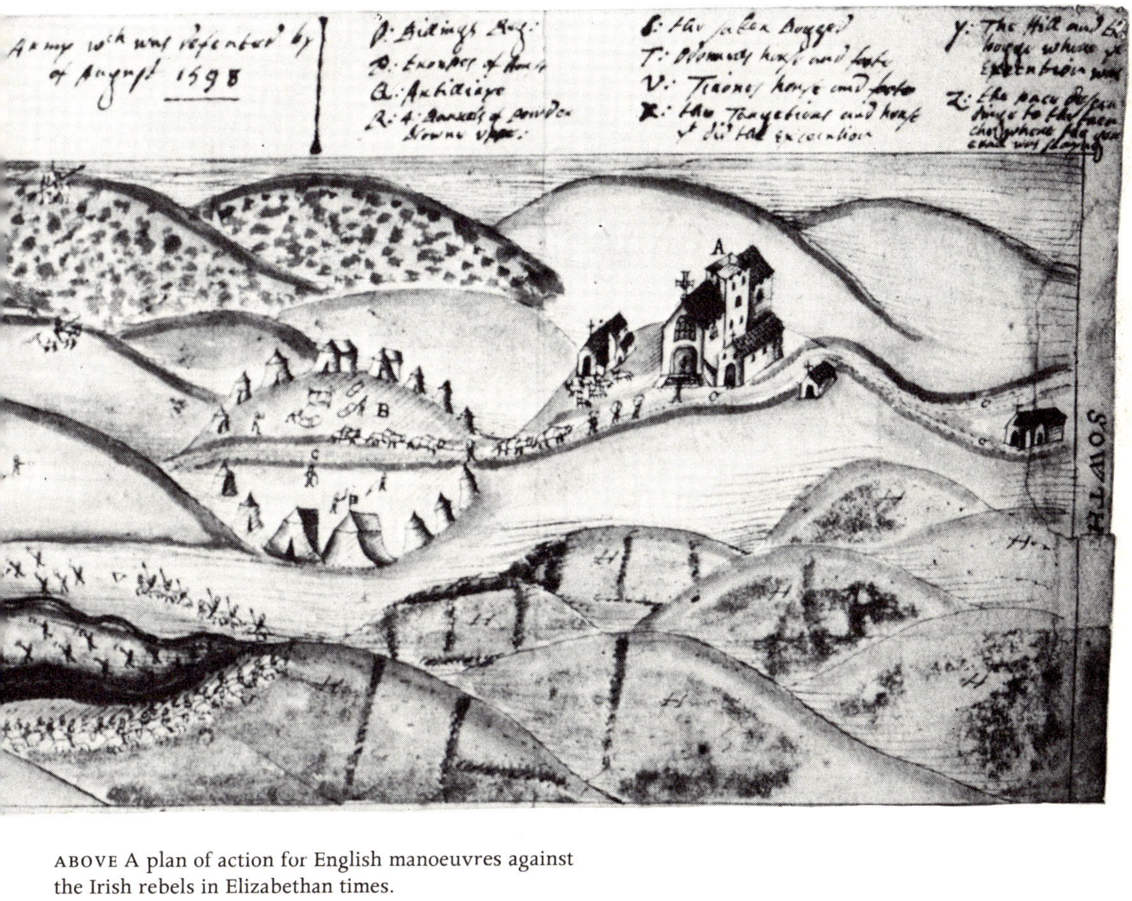

ABOVE A plan of action for English manoeuvres against the Irish rebels in Elizabethan times.

his devastation of Spanish settlements and shipping any time that he chose, and the next time, pray God, would not have the ill luck of a tropical storm or the unpleasantness of a leg injury at a crucial moment, so that he could succeed in emptying the gold from a full Treasure House at Nombre de Dios. The seas, the Spaniards and the jungle of the Isthmus had no terror for him. He could afford to be arrogant, for he had something to boast about, yet almost at once friends warned him of the changed political scene. Negotiations with Spain were now in full train to end the embargo on trade and settle damages, so this was no time to be bringing ashore plunder from the Spanish Main which could well be impounded by the government in the interests of wider commercial considerations, and Drake learned that he could well be a marked man, who might if necessary be disowned by his sovereign. He went to ground with his treasure. His bolt-hole was kept as close a secret as the entrance to 'Port Pheasant', and for nearly two years he disappears from history, as if, like his brothers Joseph and John, he had died in the Caribbean.

When Drake emerged after this mysterious period, he was in the service of Walter Devereux, Earl of Essex, who had the unenviable task of reducing the Irish rebels to English rule. Ever since O'Neill's rebellion in the early 1560s, the Hibernian bog had remained in a state of civil strife. The country was a vast no-man's-land, in which a confusion of great earldoms and petty chieftainships defied administration from Dublin Castle. One general after another had lost his reputation in attempting to 'pacify' the wretched land and Essex was ruining his health by devoted service to the Queen which earned him little thanks. We can today appreciate the full horror of Tudor Ireland, of which a contemporary wrote: 'there is no land in the world of so continual war within himself, nor of so great shedding of Christian blood, nor of so great robbing, spoiling, preying and burning, nor of so great wrongful extortions continually as in Ireland'. Spaniards, Italians and mercenaries from other Catholic powers were now serving as an international brigade to support the rebels, hoping that Ireland would become the springboard for an attack on England in which they could execute the sentence of deposing Elizabeth which Pope Pius v's bull of 1570 had proclaimed. Apparently it was Hawkins who recommended Drake to Lord Deputy Essex and (according to Stow's *Annals*) 'he did excellent service both by sea and land, at the winning of divers forts'. From 'Drake's Pool', in the neighbourhood of Cork, he lay with his ships ready to deal

OPPOSITE Sir Francis Walsingham, one of Drake's friends in high places, in a portrait after de Critz the Elder.

with any Spanish vessels attempting to land troops, and we know that he commanded the naval escorts for putting ashore English soldiers at the siege of Rathlin Island in July 1575, when John Norris massacred the garrison. Before Essex's death the following year, however, Drake had returned home.

By now the question of his surrendering his booty from the Main was largely academic, for although the Treaty of Bristol, signed in August 1574, settled the long-standing commercial disputes between English and Spanish merchants arising from the mutual confiscations and embargoes since the last days of 1568, political relations had again deteriorated, chiefly on account of Spanish successes in the Netherlands. When Drake settled again in Plymouth, he bought a house in Looe Street, opposite the Guildhall, and acquired three new vessels which he fitted out to be ready for another enterprise. This was not to be another single-handed series of raids in the Caribbean, but was envisaged as a voyage on a much grander scale, financed by a joint stock company and under royal patronage, which would certainly take in the Americas but also visit much more distant shores. His service in Ireland, far from being an unprofitable sojourn in the wilderness, had provided him with important contacts with the Court, since Essex had written a letter of introduction for him to see Sir Francis Walsingham, the Secretary of State, who was a man as staunch in his Protestantism as Drake himself and who led the war party on the Council. Moreover, his new friend Thomas Doughty, with whom he had become very close, now filled the post of secretary to Christopher Hatton, the Queen's rising favourite, and he was convinced that Hatton would do all he could to forward Drake's grand design, which was nothing less than to take an English fleet through the Strait of Magellan into the Pacific Ocean.

OPPOSITE Sir Christopher Hatton, to whom Thomas Doughty introduced Drake and who did much to further the latter's ventures.

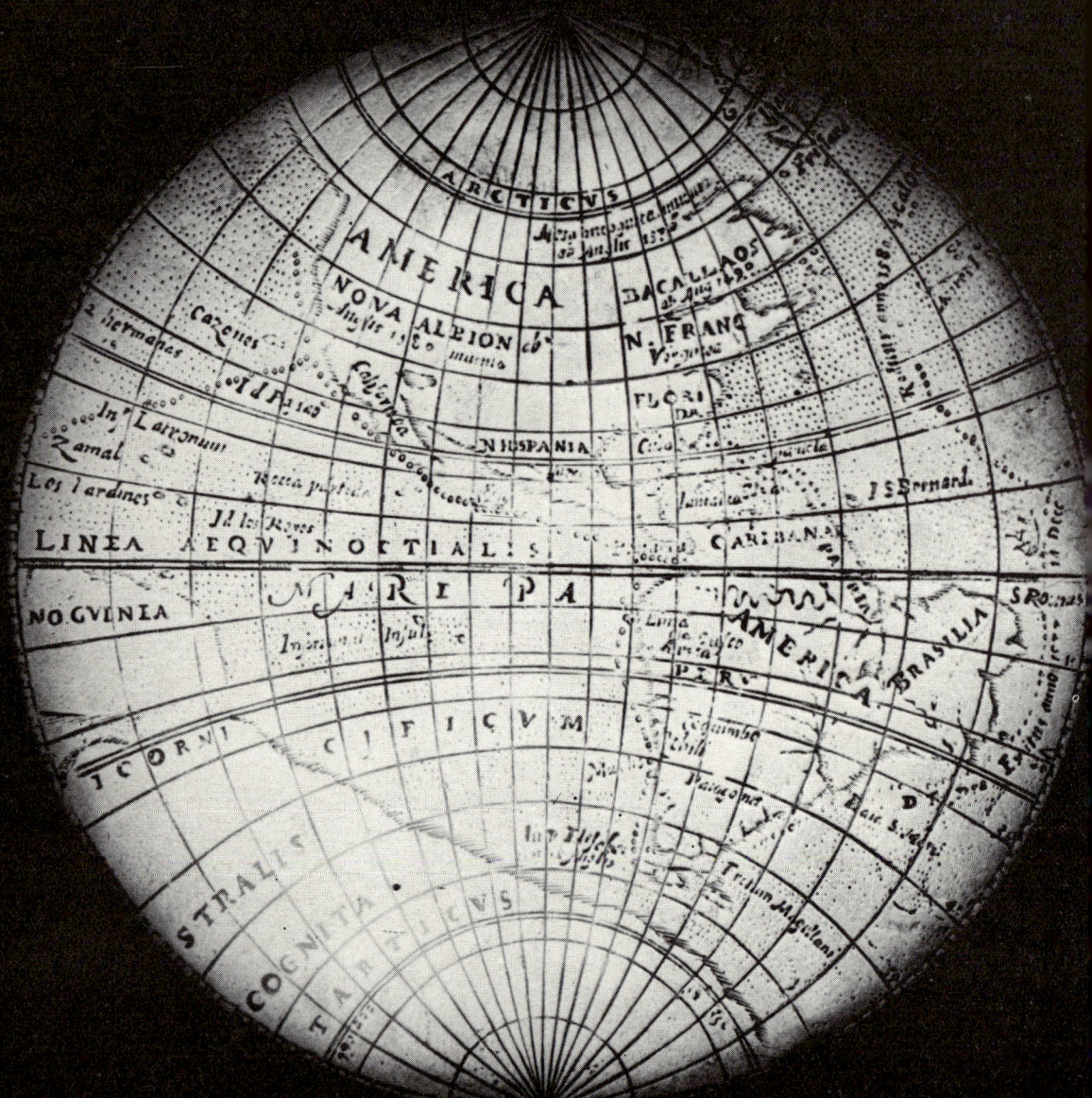

The World Encompassed

FRANCIS DRAKE HAD NEVER FORGOTTEN his dramatic glimpse of the Pacific Ocean in February 1573. It was as if he saw through a glass darkly another world, linking Panama with the East, that predicted in a glorious future another dimension to his own career. Away in Ireland and then ashore in Plymouth and London, his daydreaming gradually resolved into a practical purpose until he determined 'to sail on the same [sea] in an English bottom'. These things came to pass; and with all the problems of financing the venture and obtaining the Queen's support overcome, his expedition left England at the end of 1577. By now Drake was in his thirty-fifth year and was described as a man 'low of stature, thick-set and very robust; he has a fine countenance, is ruddy of complexion and has a fair beard'.

Since his return from the remarkable raid on Panama, Drake had become famous, as well as rich, and any scheme he suggested would be considered most seriously in high quarters. Up to a point, therefore, he scarcely needed a patron, though he welcomed the offer of Thomas Doughty whom he had come to know during his service in Ireland, to introduce him to his master, Sir Christopher Hatton. There were other straws in the wind, for Drake's interest in navigating strange waters had brought him in touch with John Dee, the mathematician and astrologer of Mortlake, who was on familiar terms with several leading courtiers, including Leicester and Walsingham, was from time to time consulted by the Queen herself and discussed the exploration of a North-West Passage with such men as Richard Hakluyt and Drake's cousin, John Hawkins, who was about to be appointed to the key post of Treasurer of the Navy.

In those years, as hostility between England and Spain became intensified, there were all kinds of plans for maritime enterprise. In 1574 Sir Richard Grenville, Drake's neighbour, was licensed to undertake a voyage for discovering 'Terra Australis', though his permit was to be cancelled for fear of Spanish reprisals. Two years later, Martin Frobisher set sail in search of the North-West Passage. It would in this climate of opinion have been a natural development for Drake to have been commissioned to voyage round the world, with the objects of attempting to found colonies in the unexplored regions of America and of furthering trade with the East Indies; and yet nothing so ambitious was projected, either by the promoters subscribing the money for the expedition or by the Queen who issued the instructions under which it operated. What Drake accomplished was something very different

PREVIOUS PAGES A map on silver from the Mercator World Map, showing Drake's route. He himself possessed such a map.

RIGHT Two illustrations from *Fragments of Ancient Shipwrighting* by Matthew Baker.
TOP Shipwrights drafting construction plans.
BOTTOM A drawing showing the construction of a ship.

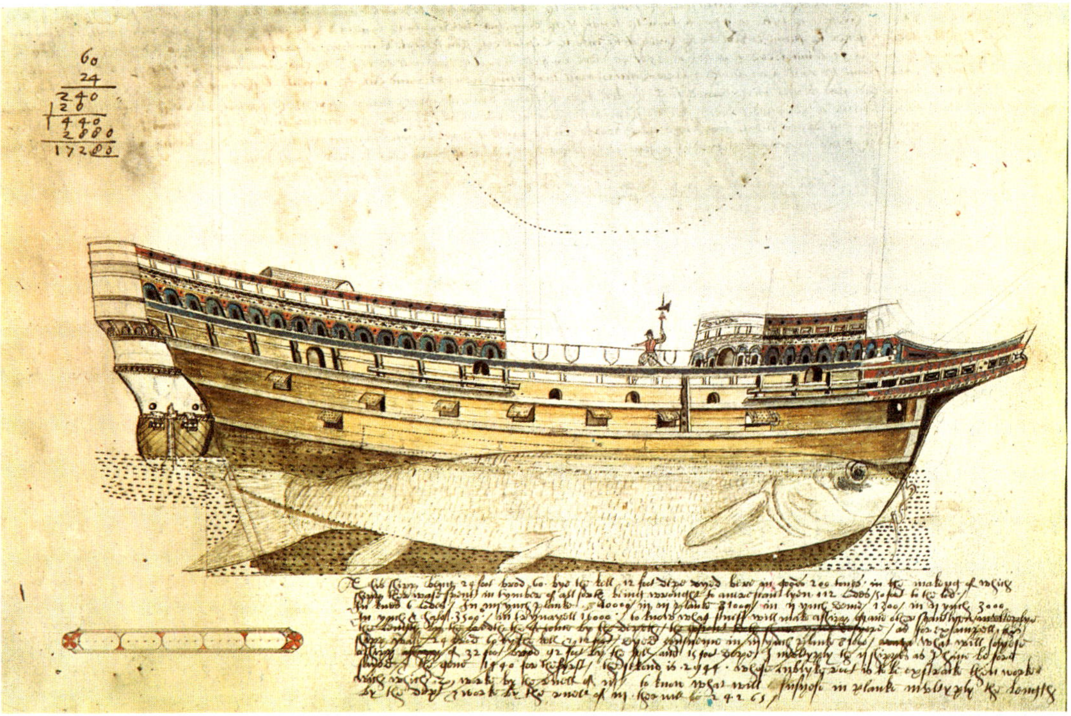

Sir Martin Frobisher, one of Drake's rivals in the world of exploration. This portrait is by Cornelius Ketel.

from the plans approved by men of more limited horizons, who had not themselves fallen under the spell of the Pacific.

We shall probably never know for certain the real intentions of the distinguished list of shareholders who backed the voyage. As a blind, it was given out that Drake was to sail to Alexandria and, certainly, most of the crews imagined this to be his destination. A document containing the draft instructions and listing the promoters has been discovered, but it is so badly damaged that the evidence in it is far from conclusive on various points. The list of names included those of the Earl of Lincoln, the Lord Admiral, the brothers Sir William and George Wynter, both senior officials of the Navy Board, and John Hawkins, whose influence on that august body was soon to be decisive – making plain the weight of official backing for Drake's project. Other even more distinguished names were those of the Earl of Leicester, Sir Francis Walsingham, the Secretary of State, and Sir Christopher Hatton, who together formed a powerful triumvirate; but a notable absentee was Burghley, Lord Treasurer of England and Elizabeth's chief minister. From this omission it has been argued that he was opposed to the venture, and even that the plans had deliberately to be kept from him by the Queen. But his name *may* have featured at the head of the list, where the page is now defective; and even if he was never associated with the others in financing the voyage, there is all the difference in the world between the cautious Burghley's not wanting to invest in an enterprise in which there was a strong element of risk and his unwillingness to endorse a policy which might lead to a further deterioration of relations with Spain. Thomas Doughty has been said by some to have been planted on the expedition as Burghley's spy, which ill accords with his role as Hatton's man. Much, too, has been built on the account (by Cooke) of what Drake said at Doughty's trial: that Walsingham had introduced Drake to the Queen, who urged him to undertake an expedition to revenge her injuries on the King of Spain by annoying him 'in his Indies'.

Certainly Drake's authority was supreme, yet there is no reason for thinking that he had reached an understanding with Queen Elizabeth, kept a close secret from other promoters, that the main object of the voyage was to attack Spain's shipping and settlements. Of course, everyone in the venture knew from Drake's past performance and his character that he would take every opportunity that came his way for plundering, but these were to be fringe benefits. Circumnavigation of the globe, the discovery of

QVÆ NATVRA POTEST HATTONO CONTVLIT VNI;
ET FORTVNA DEDIT, QVÆ DARE, CVNCTA, POTEST;
CERTATIM VIRTVS CVMVLVM SVPERADDIDIT ISTIS;
ANGLICA DIVA TAMEN PLVS TRIBVS VNA DEDIT.
ECQVID HABENT TANTAM SATVRNIA SECVLA DIVAM?
ECQVID HABENT TALEM TEMPORA NOSTRA VIRVM?

'Terra Australis' (a project of Grenville's so recently abandoned by royal command), the annexation of New Albion on the coast of California and the foundation of English interests in the Spice Islands were not at all in the minds of the Queen, Hatton or the others; yet they knew that the opportunist captain would not overlook any course of action that would be advantageous to his shareholders or bring credit to his Queen. Basically, his instructions were to reconnoitre the coast of South America from the River Plate right round Cape Horn to the region in Chile at which Spanish occupation stopped; settlement and a long-term conquest of Spanish Peru was envisaged and in the view of at least one man (the younger Hakluyt) this would 'subject to England all the golden mines of Peru and all the coast' of America upon that sea.

In the event, Francis Drake did not deflect the voyage from its agreed purpose and was to spend two months on the east coast of South America south of 32° South, and two further months at Port St Julian. Then, after enduring a terrific gale in the region of the Strait of Magellan, he was to spend two months on the west coast, between 39° and 28°S. What happened afterwards depended on the weather and the state of his ship and crew, but 'was fully justified by the dangerous weather conditions on the recommended return route and by the generally unpromising results of his reconnaissance'. In the surviving fragment of his draft instructions, Drake was empowered to decide how far north to proceed along the coast of Chile, and he must have had full discretion to amend his route thereafter.

On 15 November 1577 the fleet sailed from Plymouth, with Drake flying his flag in the *Pelican*, later to be renamed the *Golden Hind*. Though no exact drawings or measurements of the vessel survive, a great many details about her have come down to us. She was a small galleon, small even by sixteenth-century standards, being not more than 140 tons. She carried three masts – the main and the foremast being square-rigged, with topsails, spritsails and top-gallants, and a lateen sail on the mizzen; the total sail area was 4,150 square feet. There was a low forecastle and an after-castle which was higher, so that head-on the ship seemed unstable to a land-lubber. The *Pelican* was well-armed, with seven guns under hatches on each side, two in the poop and a number of smaller cannon. She was about 100 feet long, 18 feet in the beam and had a draught, fully-laden, of 13 feet.

The Portuguese pilot, Nuño da Silva, who spent fifteen months aboard, noted with a practised eye: 'Drake's ship is very stout and

OPPOSITE The arms of Sir Christopher Hatton: Drake took the emblem of the hind and renamed the *Pelican* the *Golden Hind* in honour of his patron.

very strong, with double sheathings. . . . She is a French ship, well-fitted with good masts, tackle and good sails, and is a good sailer, answering the helm well. She is neither new, nor is her bottom covered with lead. . . . She is staunch when sailing with the wind astern if it is not very strong, but in a sea which makes her labour she makes no little water.' It was a vessel of which da Silva was indeed envious, and he was fascinated by the stores and facilities provided, not least the forge for making nails. The Portuguese probably meant that the *Pelican* was built 'after the French fashion', not that she had been constructed in France. Some have thought that she was built at Deptford, where she finally came to rest, but if so, it was very remarkable that once she had become the most famous ship in the world no English shipwright should have come forward to advertise his craftsmanship.

Drake's crew numbered ninety, of whom nine were 'gentlemen, younger sons of English land-owning families'. There was room in the small forecastle for only a few of the crew, and most seamen slept on the gun deck. The officers slept in cabins aft, as was customary, and fed together in the Great Cabin, while the musicians played, with the captain's chair at the head of the table. Drake intended to live in style afloat, with goodly provision 'for ornament and delight, carrying to this purpose with him expert musicians, rich furniture . . . whereby the civility and magnificence of his native country might amongst all nations, whithersoever he should come, be the more admired'. His own cabin was panelled in oak. Besides a bed and a chair, there was a desk and a table on which he kept charts, books and instruments, and also his sea-chest covered in leather, which is still to be seen at Berkeley Castle in Gloucestershire, with the inside of the lid painted with views of his vessel. Here, too, was the captain's drum, on which was painted his arms, of which he was intensely proud, for they decorated his plates and some of his guns; da Silva noted that on one bronze cannon 'was sculptured the globe of the world with a north star over it, passing over. He [Drake] said these were his arms and that the Queen had conferred them upon him, commanding him to encompass the world.' The Captain had rather jumped the gun, if he spoke as da Silva reported, for his grant to bear arms was not issued until after his return home! Among his books was a copy of *Magellan's Voyages*. 'Francis Drake', wrote the Portuguese, 'kept a book in which he entered his navigations and in which he delineated birds, trees and sea-lions. He is adept at painting, and with him' his nephew John, 'who is a great painter. When they both shut themselves up in his cabin they are always painting.' There was a practical purpose in this recreation, for uncle and nephew sketched coastlines, harbours and islands not as imaginative seascapes, but as a faithful record to illustrate 'sailing directions'.

Five ships sailed in company, manned by 164 men, but only the *Pelican* completed the circumnavigation. When Magellan had set out on his voyage in September 1519, there had also been a fleet of five, and then, too, only the flagship returned safely to port, though without the admiral. In 1577 the other four English craft were the *Elizabeth* of eighty tons under John Wynter, Vice-Admiral, the *Swan*, a flyboat of fifty tons captained by John Chester, the *Marigold*, a bark of thirty tons commanded by John Thomas and the tiny *Christopher*, a pinnace of perhaps only fifteen tons, under Thomas Moone. It seems incredible that such small vessels were journeying into such distant, unknown waters, but as yet only Drake knew the destination. There was a stiff breeze blowing when they sailed past Rame Head in the late afternoon and by dawn, when they were off the Lizard, this had developed into a howling gale so the ships had to take shelter in Falmouth. Despite the protection of the harbour, both the *Pelican* and the *Marigold* were in trouble, especially with their masts, and after the storm had abated, Drake decided to return to Plymouth, arriving there thirteen days after he had originally set out. It was an inauspicious beginning. During the next fortnight, repairs were successfully completed and then, on 13 December, the fleet made a second attempt, 'holding on with a prosperous wind and good success in all things', bound for the Barbary Coast in North Africa. The only mishap was when a ship's boy was lost overboard from the *Christopher* off Portugal.

On Christmas Day they arrived at the island of Mogador, part of the dominions of the Moorish kingdom of Fez, that had not so long before been under Portuguese rule. Here one of the men, John Fry, who had picked up something of the local language from an earlier trading voyage, indiscreetly went ashore and was taken captive. Drake led a posse to try to rescue the unfortunate man, but had to give him up for lost; Fry was subsequently released and sent home in a Mediterranean trader. The fleet passed on south, taking two Spanish caravels near the Tropic of Cancer, and raced towards Cape Blanco on the Moroccan Coast, with 'every sail at command, as if Neptune had been present'. At the Cape, Drake stayed for six days to water and clean his ships and here he left

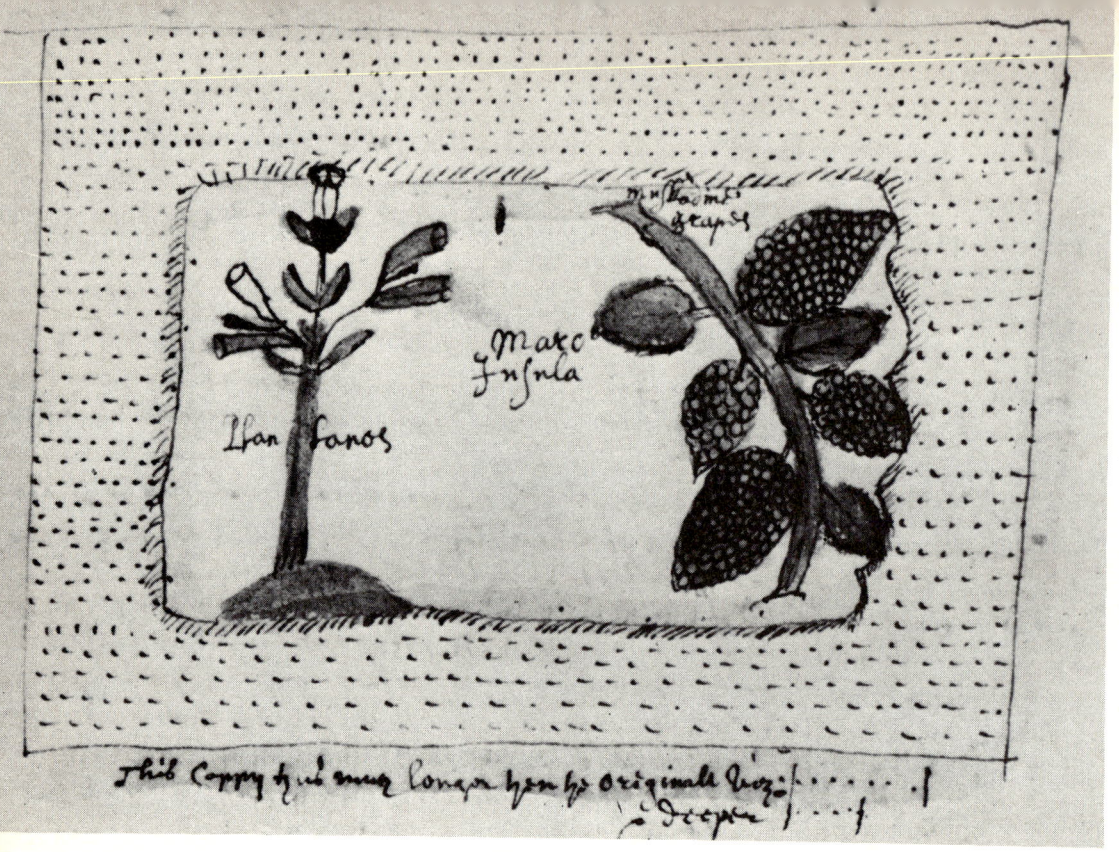

ABOVE Maio, one of the Cape Verde Islands, drawn by Francis Fletcher, Drake's chaplain aboard the *Golden Hind*.

OPPOSITE Another of Fletcher's sketches showing the coast of West Africa and some of the fish encountered in these seas.

behind the pinnace *Christopher*, which he replaced by one of the captured caravels, renamed *Christopher* out of deference to Sir Christopher Hatton's interest in the expedition. The Cape Verde Islands, near the mouth of the River Gambia, were the next port of call and here, early in February, they took a Portuguese ship, bound for Brazil with a cargo of wine and cloth, which Drake added to his fleet as the *Mary*. Portuguese vessels had been fair game for English privateers 'over the Line', but hitherto there had been an uneasy peace in other waters. Drake had no qualms about taking the prize and before he could return to England, Portugal would be invaded and conquered by Spain.

More important than the capture of the *Mary* was the acquisition of her pilot, Nuño da Silva, whom Drake pressed into his service. He was a most experienced navigator and the English Captain was fascinated by his collection of charts and nautical instruments. Nuño was to stay aboard the *Pelican*, where he was honourably treated, feeding at the Captain's table, for some fifteen months. By now Drake had divulged to his officers that he intended to sail into the Pacific, and the Portuguese pilot caught the adventurous spirit of his captor 'to travel unto the new-discovered parts of the world'. Da Silva's experience of the South Atlantic was consider-

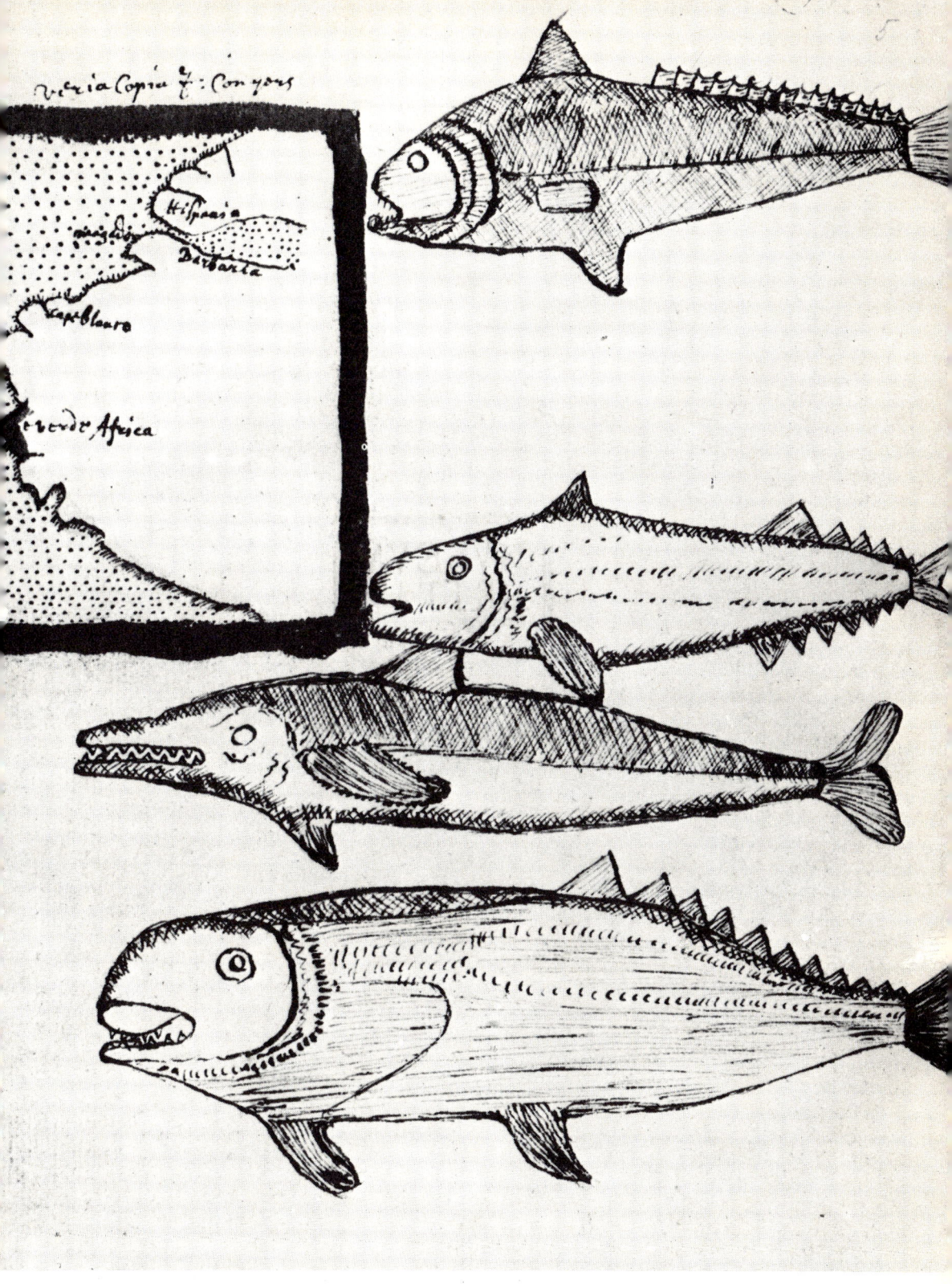

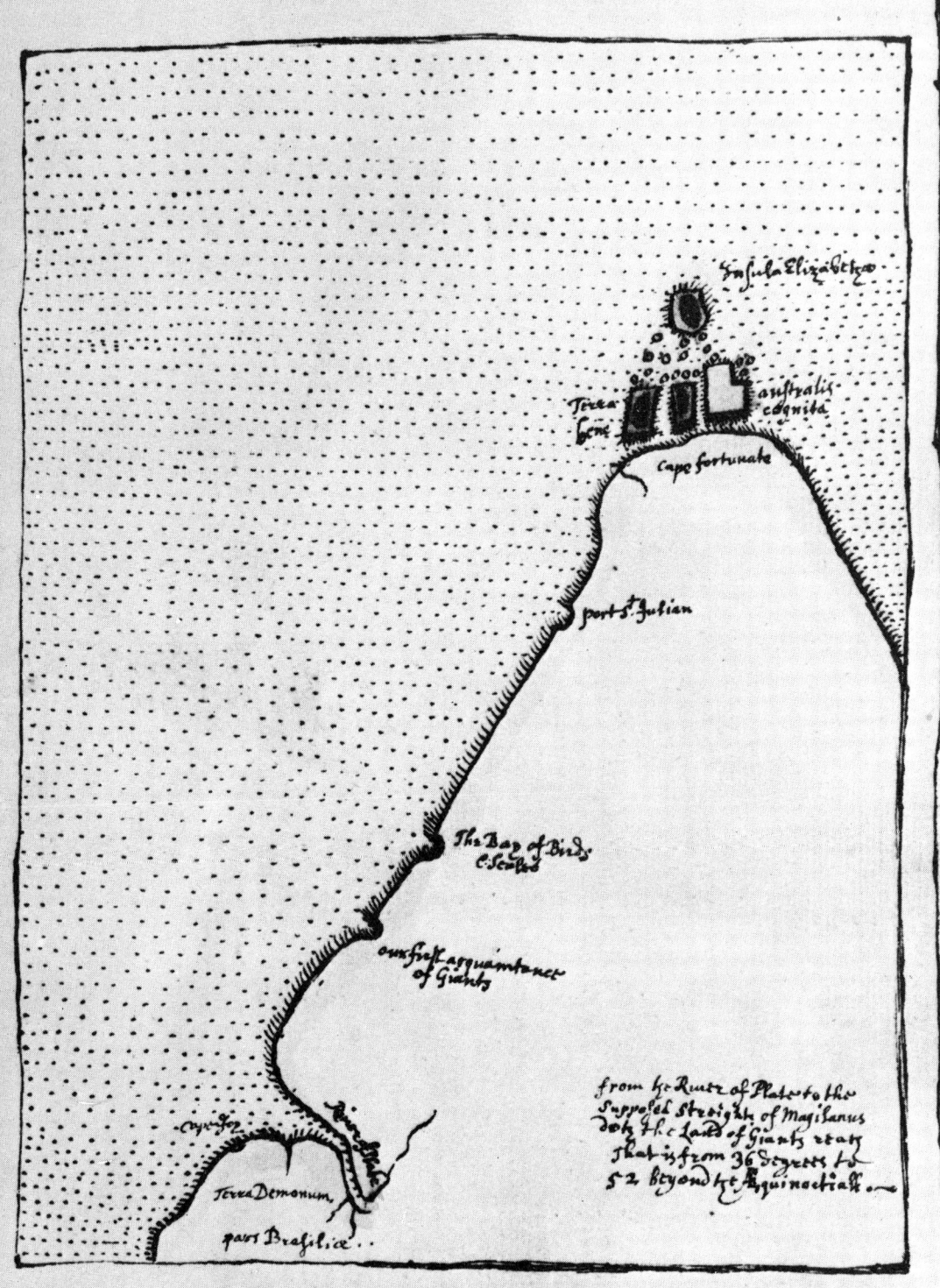

able and once they reached the South American coast he displayed detailed knowledge.

In the 'southern seas', when they had crossed the Equator, conditions were eerie; the climate was fickle and in the Doldrums a flat calm under the burning sun could be followed without warning by a sudden tempest. The sight of strange birds and tropical fish alarmed the superstitious, while crossing the line itself was something that made many feel uneasy. Some of the crew were on edge, questioning the route, the destination and even the ability of their admiral. Thomas Doughty, the courtier, had been placed in command of the Portuguese prize, but from the first there had been trouble, when he falsely accused Drake's youngest brother, serving as an ordinary mariner, of tampering with the cargo. Later, Doughty and Francis Drake exchanged commands. When the ships were in the Doldrums, Drake learned from the trumpeter, John Brewer, that Doughty had made a seditious speech attempting to persuade his crew to desert, and so he made him a prisoner in the *Swan* on charges of mutiny and witchcraft. Doughty certainly believed in the occult. Some feared that he was a spy in Spanish pay, others that he was an agent of Lord Burghley's, a few that he was a coward as well as a landlubber. Naturally he found supporters who either shared his lack of confidence in Drake or were lukewarm about the great adventure on which they had embarked without being aware of the secret plans.

After two months without sight of land, the fleet reached the South American coast, to the north of the River Plate. It was truly a relief to see land again, for it brought the promise of fresh provisions and water and the chance of careening the ships. Then suddenly the ships were engulfed by a thick fog 'with the palpable darkness of Egypt' and this was followed by the most terrific storm Drake had ever known. The *Pelican* was in danger of being driven on to a lee shore and only the Portuguese pilot's skill and local knowledge of shoals saved her. So near a disaster had provoked Thomas Doughty into stirring up fresh trouble in the *Swan*. He told the crew that but for his own influence with important investors, Drake would never have succeeded in sailing. Dinner-table talk about mutineers led one officer to aver that Drake should deal with such as Magellan did, 'which was to hang them up to be an example'. 'Nay, soft!' Doughty retorted. 'His authority is none such as Magellan's was, for I know his authority so well as he himself doth.' As the discussions continued, it was clear that the trouble-maker was endeavouring to

OPPOSITE A skilful drawing by Fletcher of the tip of South America, showing Elizabeth Island just by the Strait of Magellan.

undermine Drake's position and even to stir men to mutiny.

As they went down the coast of Brazil, it proved impossible to keep the little fleet together and Drake spent many days sailing up and down to find stragglers, or those who had parted company; he would not rest until he had found them all. The *Swan* was becoming too much of a liability (quite apart from Doughty) and so the crew and provisions were transferred to the *Pelican*, and the flyboat, after the cannons and iron-work had been removed, was abandoned in Seal Bay in Patagonia. A little later on, Drake similarly laid up the *Christopher II*. Near Port St Julian, not so far from the Strait of Magellan, the missing ship, the *Mary*, at last came into sight on 18 June 1578 and Drake decided that it would be wisest to abandon her. There was still an ominous undercurrent of sedition, yet everyone knew that St Julian was the place at which Magellan had executed his mutineers in 1520. Ashore the Englishmen found the remains of the fir-wood gibbet and, with a devilish sense of the macabre, a cooper from the *Pelican* made tankards from the gibbet's wood.

A target was set up on land for archery practice in which two Patagonians joined, but a fight developed when other natives arrived, and two Englishmen were killed. These casualties were a blow for morale, which was already at a low ebb, and Drake felt that he could no longer turn a blind eye to the behaviour of Thomas Doughty. His drum summoned every man ashore for a traditional trial and, before a jury of forty, various witnesses were heard and the prisoner was given leave to address the court. In his speech, Doughty claimed that he was the real architect of the expedition, in persuading the Queen of its feasibility, and shared equal authority with Drake, who had consistently ignored him and had not even been straightforward with him about the true destination of the fleet. Drake answered these points briefly and made known to all that Queen Elizabeth had given him a sword, to use for his personal safety, telling him, 'We do account that he which striketh at thee, Drake, striketh at us.' The jury pronounced the prisoner guilty and deserving of death as a mutineer, and Drake thereupon gave him the customary choice – to be marooned ashore, to be executed forthwith or to be taken home in chains to appear in due course before the Privy Council. Next day Doughty made it known that he chose execution, as befitting a gentleman, he added. Before sentence, at his request, Drake and he took the sacrament together and then, as was customary, all the officers entertained him to a banquet. Afterwards the two protagonists

OPPOSITE Two of Drake's raids in the Caribbean, from Boazzio's set of engravings: the advance of his ships on Santiago (TOP); his attack on Cartagena (BOTTOM).

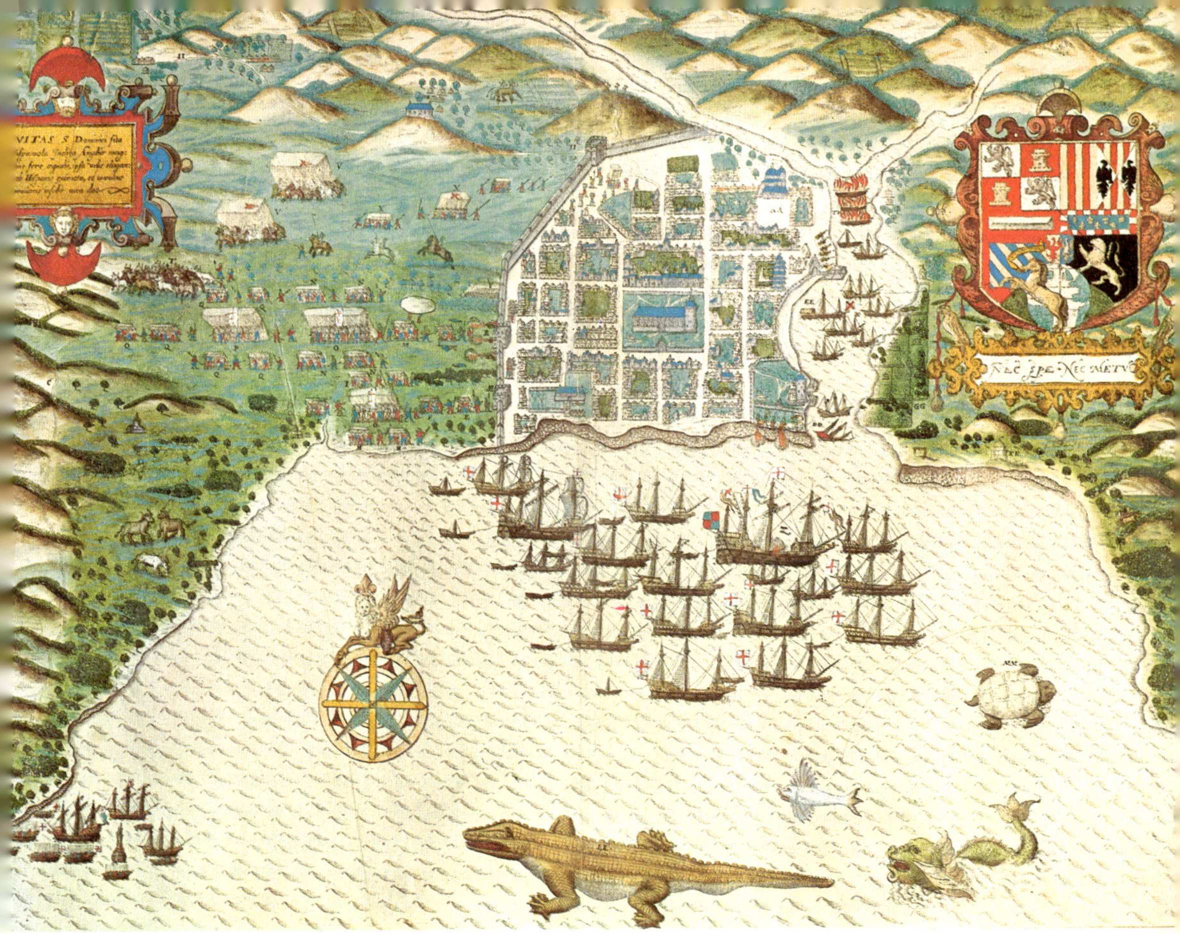

CIVITAS S. DOMINICI

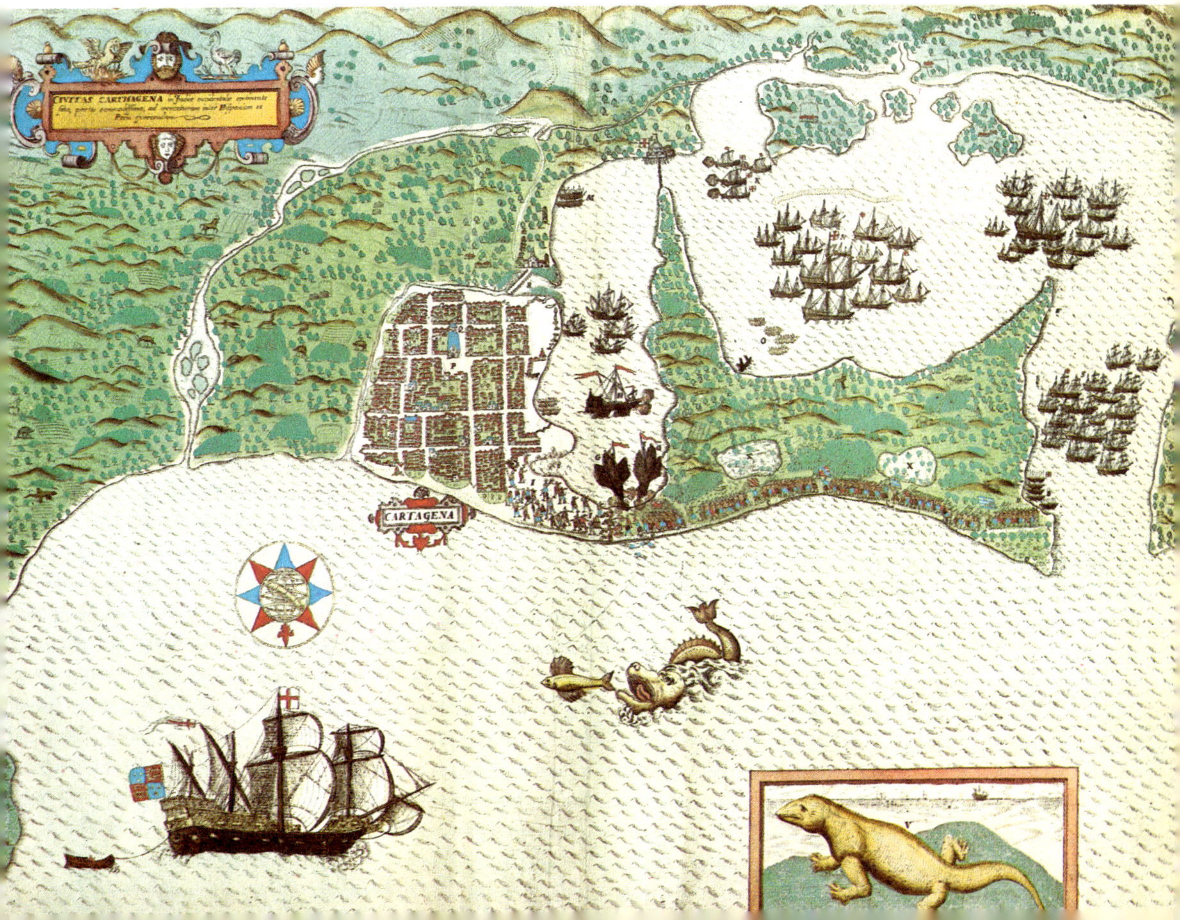

CIVITAS CARTHAGENA

talked together in secret in Drake's cabin and we may assume that Doughty made confession of his faults. Certainly, the fact that he deliberately chose not to face trial in England, despite his contacts with men in high places, suggests that his conduct had been indefensible. Although we shall never know the extent of his crime, for all contemporary accounts are partial, we can readily appreciate the strain under which Drake was placed, for Doughty had been his friend. Doughty's conduct had in his view put the entire expedition in jeopardy and there could be no hope of success while he lived. The man had to be sacrificed on the altar of naval discipline. As the severed head fell from the block, Drake picked it up, exclaiming 'Look, this is the end of traitors.' He was buried ashore.

There were still murmurings, and to silence any further factions Drake's drum rolled out once more to summon every man ashore. They stood in ranks in front of a tent, set up at Port St Julian, with Drake flanked by Captain Thomas of the *Marigold* and Captain Wynter of the *Elizabeth*. In a forceful, emotional speech, Drake talked of the dangers that lay ahead and threatened any who made for disunity, rather than making a plea for unity. From papers in his hand, he scotched the theory which Doughty had put forward about the origins of the voyage and about his own authority as commander. He told them of the Queen's summons to her presence: '"Drake, so it is that I would gladly be revenged on the King of Spain for divers injuries I have received", and said further that I was the only man [who] might do the exploit.' Doughty, he said, was not alone in his treachery and he now named others who knelt for pardon; they were assured that 'there shall be no more deaths'. He then astounded his hearers by announcing that *all* his officers were dismissed from their posts. They protested in vain, for this son of a Devonshire nobody made it plain to them that he would stomach no class distinctions at sea. In this adventure the ordinary seaman and the courtier were of equal rank, and they must share in the dirty jobs, be equally subject to the hazards of the waves and the dangers from enemies, and learn to pull together in every way. 'My masters, I must have it left. I must have the gentleman to haul and draw with the mariner, and the mariner with the gentleman, I would know him that would refuse to set his hand to a rope.' They had sailed of their own free will, they were not pressed men and if any now wanted to change his mind he would do his best to find him a passage home; but if any such crossed his course he would send him to the bottom. This sermon went home and they left the 'Island of Blood' in better spirits on 17 August, 'being now in great hope of a happy issue to our enterprise'. His personal magnetism no less than his preaching had made every member of the crews conscious of his superb leadership.

Three days later, as they passed Cape Virgins, almost at the entrance to the Strait of Magellan, the perilous gateway to the unknown, Drake stage-managed a ceremony which raised his men's spirits. He caused his little fleet, now reduced to three vessels, to strike their topsails as an act of homage to the Queen, in token of their obedience to her and their recognition of her personal interest in their exploits. At the same time, in honour of his friend and sponsor Sir Christopher Hatton, Drake changed the name of his ship from the *Pelican* to the *Golden Hind*, taken from Hatton's coat of arms. He instructed his nephew John to embellish the vessel with Hatton's arms and to paint the stern in the red and yellow of his livery, while the ship's carpenter made a figurehead of a hind to take the place of the pelican. Nuño da Silva thought that young John Drake had the qualities of a Leonardo.

Magellan had taken thirty-seven days to traverse the Strait named after him, but Drake took only sixteen. On the fourth day, they named an island they came to after St George, their patron saint. They killed penguins – birds 'less than a goose, but bigger than a mallard', wrote Chaplain Fletcher – to supplement their food and felled a massive tree, stored in the hold as ballast, with the intention of presenting it to the Queen, 'as a sign they had passed the Strait'. The ships faced a strong headwind in the second half of the passage, because the high shores acted as a tunnel for the wind. Once they entered the South Sea on 6 September, Drake intended mustering his company ashore and, after preaching to them, to have set up on the land 'a monument of her majesty engraven in metal', yet there was no hope of the vessels finding a safe anchorage. Coming into the South Sea, the little ships faced a terrific gale, which lasted a full month and before it had blown itself out, the *Marigold* became detached from the others and was lost. As Wynter put it, 'that night was the most tempestuous night that ever was seen in this outrageous weather'. During this gale, Drake was beaten well to the south of Cape Horn, much to his dismay, yet this enabled him to make the discovery that there was no continent stretching from the Antarctic, as had been supposed, and instead there was open sea to the south of South America, a merger of Atlantic and Pacific. Coming again along the coast,

Drake anchored but lost his cable, and then the *Golden Hind* lost touch with the *Elizabeth,* Wynter's ship. Fires were lit ashore to attract attention, but to no avail. Wynter himself feared that Drake's vessel may have been wrecked and decided that the best plan would be for him to re-enter Magellan's Strait and turn eastwards towards the Moluccas, where he might happily *rendezvous* with his admiral, for Drake had told him that they would eventually make for the Spice Islands. As it happened, Wynter had too much difficulty in persuading his crew not to return from their hazardous voyage and instead of sailing east he made for England, arriving in June 1579 to announce that the *Marigold* had been wrecked and perhaps the *Golden Hind* as well.

Meanwhile, having repaired the *Golden Hind* after the storm, Drake found fairer weather. He made his way up the coast of Chile and made a stop at the Island of Mocha, a most fruitful place, but the Indian inhabitants, mostly refugees from Spanish colonial rule, attacked the English landing party as they were admiring the ostriches. Drake was shot by arrows in the right cheek, under his right eye and close by his nose – a very narrow escape – and da Silva in chronicling the event mentioned his old war wound: 'In one leg he has an arquebus ball that was shot at him in the Indies.' Four of the crew had fallen in the Indians' attack and another ten were badly wounded. As soon as they were able, they continued their northerly cruise, for Drake fervently hoped that he might make contact with John Oxenham and his men for an eventual attack on Panama. But *en route* there came all kinds of opportunities and the attack on Valparaiso was like old times for they took 25,000 gold pesos from a Chilean vessel in the port on 5 December.

Drake was to devote the next four weeks to a series of intrepid raids on Spanish settlements ashore and craft afloat, varied only by a short period of careening in a safe bay. Early in February 1579 he took a quantity of silver at Arica, but unfortunately missed a rich cargo at Chule, which was stored safely ashore by the Spaniards in the nick of time. A day or so later, he reached Callao, the chief port of Peru, and towards midnight he took the *Golden Hind* into harbour to anchor in the middle of some thirty vessels. No warning had been sent to the Viceroy about the likelihood of Drake's descent, but at first light the terrified Spanish realised the identity of their companion. As the ships cut their moorings, to drift about the harbour, Drake concentrated on boarding from his pinnace the largest vessel in search of treasure. Aboard they found a black leathern chest crammed full of 'royals of plate'. Next they

OPPOSITE Another detail of the assault on Santiago.

OVERLEAF PAGES One of the most alarming experiences of the Circumnavigation for Drake: Indians attacking him at the Island of Mocha. An illustration from de Bry's *Grand Voyages*.

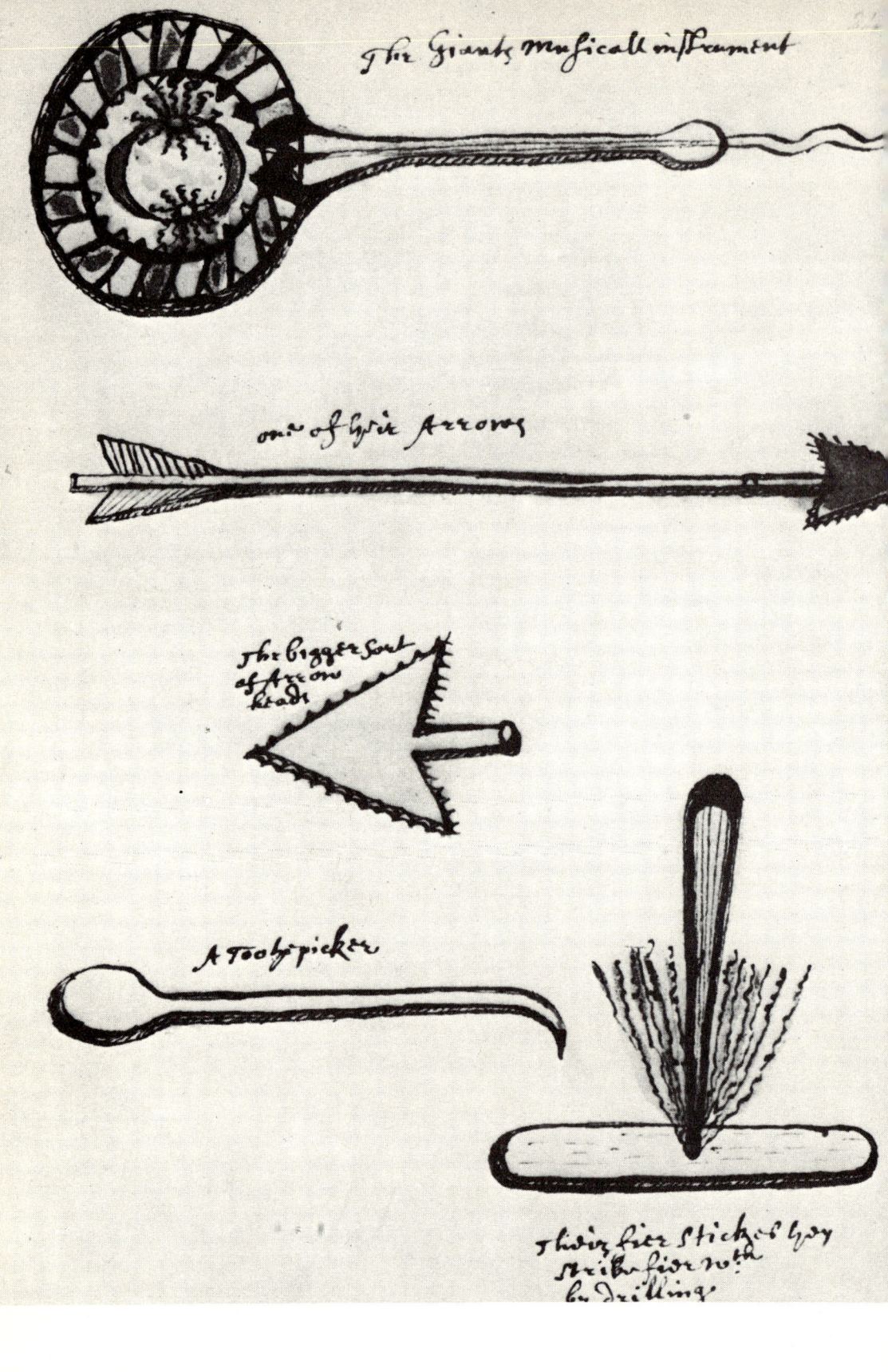

attacked the *San Cristobel* newly arrived from Panama and easily seized her. But Drake had to abandon the plan dear to his heart for rescuing his old shipmate, Oxenham, who lay a prisoner of the Inquisition at Lima, not far inland from Callao. Had he possessed a stronger force (including Wynter's men), he would have marched inland but now he could only hope that his show of strength in the harbour would lead the Inquisition to spare John Oxenham's life, and he wrote to the Viceroy to the effect that the man's execution would lead to terrible reprisals. Drake was anxious to be away, partly because he sensed that it could not be long before a Spanish fleet was sent after him, but even more because he had picked up information in Callao that further south was a large vessel with a fabulous cargo – none other than the *Cacafuego, en route* from Lima to Panama. He put out all his canvas to give chase and a fortnight later, on the afternoon of St David's Day, he came up with her.

OPPOSITE Items belonging to the 'Giants' as Fletcher called some of the natives: a musical instrument, an arrow, an arrowhead, a toothpick and an implement used to produce fire.

LEFT Fletcher's view of the Island of Mocha.

Artist Aboard the Golden Hind

Francis Fletcher's record of Drake's circumnavigation survives in the manuscript of his book in the Sloane Collection in the British Museum. Here is a selection of the fascinating sketches of this unusual cleric, briefly excommunicated by Drake for the sake of naval discipline.

BELOW LEFT The island of Fogo, one of the Cape Verde complex.
BELOW A typical boat of the South Sea Islands.

RIGHT A duck 'like foule' observed by Fletcher.

A frosen mountaine
wth Regions of Ise
& snow about it
never dissolved
by anny heat of
the Sonn.
32

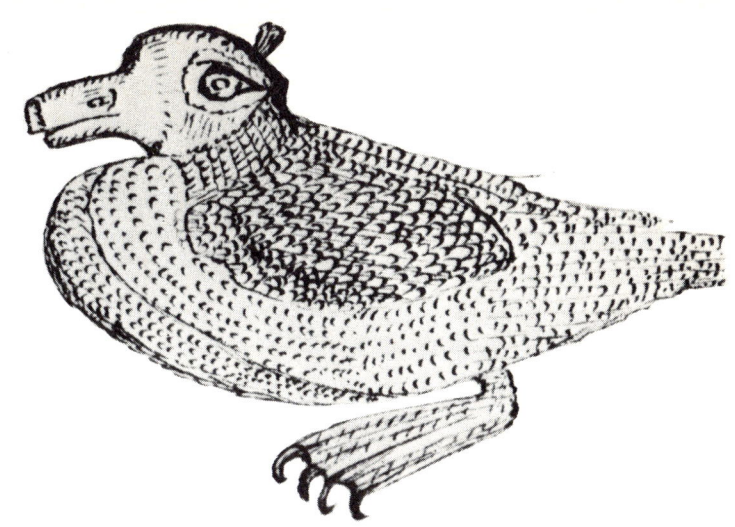

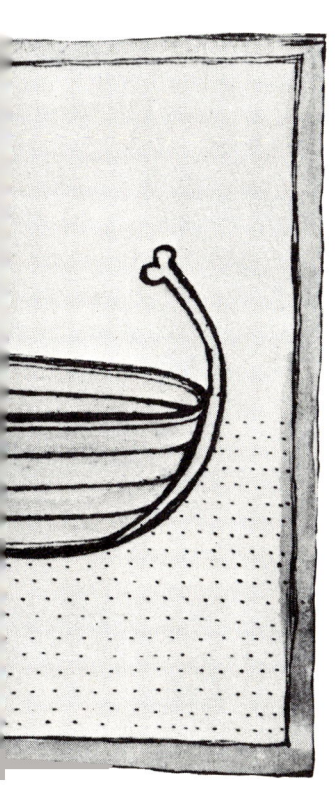

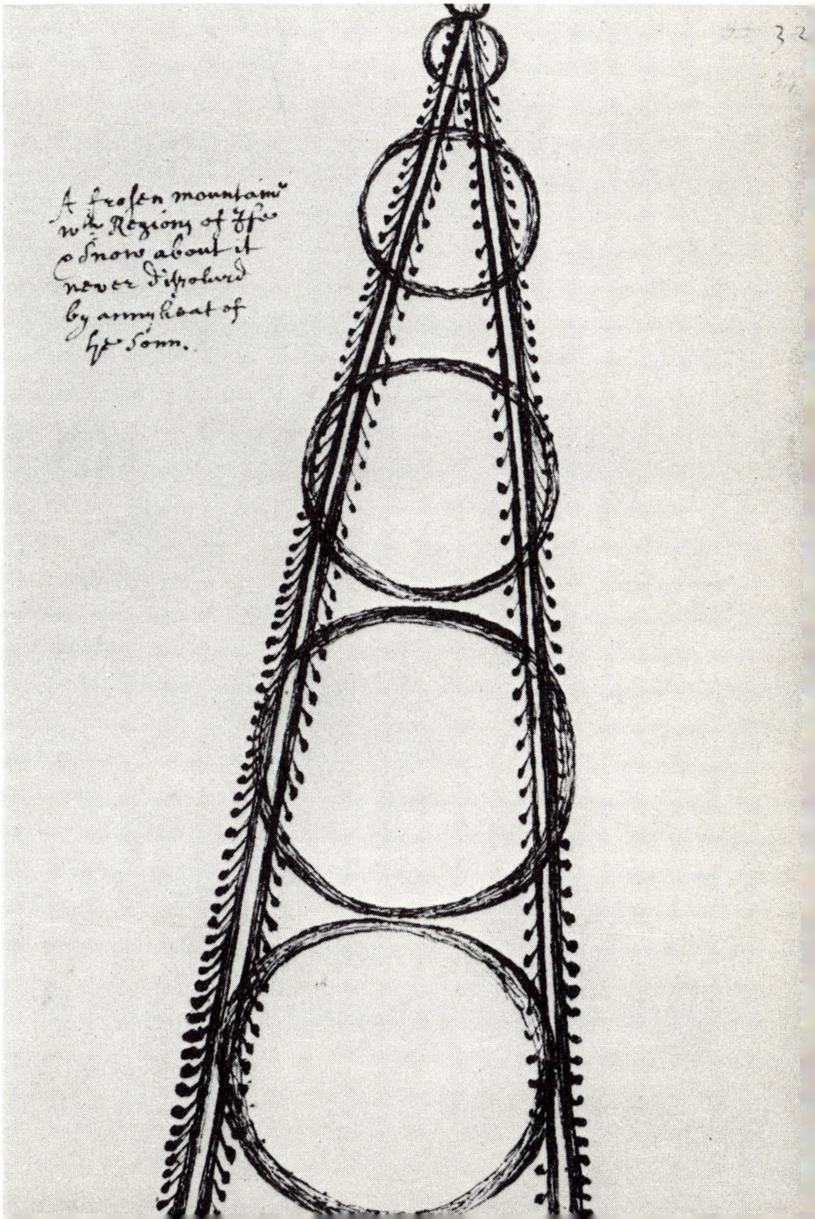

RIGHT A 'frozen mountain' (iceberg) in the Strait of Magellan.

The *Golden Hind* drawing alongside the *Cacafuego* after a hot chase.

Her true name was the *Nuestra Señora de la Concepción*; for *Cacafuego* was a somewhat obscene nickname coined on the lower deck of a Spanish galleon. Drake knew that she was a floating treasure-house and offered a gold chain to the man who should spot her first; the winner was his hawk-eyed nephew John, who was in the crow's nest. Young Drake subsequently wore his prize chain from his neck. By a masterful ruse, the Admiral succeeded in giving the Spaniards the impression that the *Golden Hind* was not a fast ship. He left all her sail unfurled, but towed astern cables, mattresses and even heavy pots. When it got dark, he cut adrift these tows, quickly overtook the great ship, which had never considered herself in danger, and lowering his sails was ready to come alongside. To the Spanish captain's question, 'What ship is this?' came the shout, '*Nuestra Señora de la Concepción*, we are English! Strike sail, or we send you to the bottom!' 'What English? Who does bid me strike sail? Never. Come aboard and strike sail yourself.' Drake opened fire. His first shot carried away the mizzen mast, his second damaged the rigging by the mainmast. Under cover of a volley of musket shots, the pinnace came alongside the *Cacafuego* and the English boarding-party soon took command of the vessel. The captain, San Juan de Anton, and his boatswain were brought aboard the *Golden Hind* as Drake was removing his helmet and coat of mail; he told the Spaniards 'Be patient, for such is the usage of war' and then took them to his cabin. Aboard the prize, all crew and passengers were closely guarded while the great ship was moved well away from prying eyes ashore to an isolated stretch of sheltered water. Here, over six days, the rich cargo was transferred to the hold of the *Golden Hind*. It comprised, runs the Englishmen's report, 'fruits, conserves, sugars and a great quantity of jewels and precious stones, 13 chests of royals of plate, 80 lb weight of gold [and] 26 tons of uncoined silver'. It was a staggering array of booty.

Drake talked freely with San Juan de Anton, telling him that he had come 'to rob by command of the Queen of England and carried the arms she had given him and her commission'. He also made plain his concern for Oxenham and his fellow prisoners at Lima and said, 'Tell the Viceroy of Peru not to hang them, for if he does I swear it will cost the heads of 3,000 men of Peru, all of which heads I will cast into the port of Callao.' This message was in fact delivered and prolonged Oxenham's life, though the next year, when Drake had left American waters, the prisoners of the Inquisition went to their execution. Drake had been bent on showing the Spaniards an Englishman's clemency to captives and put the men from the *Cacafuego* ashore, even providing Anton with credentials to show to Wynter, should he meet with him, to be let off lightly.

After the capture of the *Cacafuego*, subsequent prizes would necessarily come as an anti-climax, yet the Spanish authorities had no idea where Drake would strike next, and they perused maps trying to anticipate his movements once he had left the Peruvian coast. One thought that he would navigate 'very far north' to look for the North-West passage home, since 'a man who has had the spirit to do what he has done will not be lacking in courage to persevere in his attempt'. Such was, indeed, Drake's long-term plan, but immediately he looked to Nicaragua. Off that coast he took a bark bound for Panama and though he set the crew ashore, he kept the pilot, who had with him a fine collection of charts, including some for the China route, since the man was to pick up a vessel at Panama to navigate her to the Moluccas. Next he captured the *Espirito Santo* off Guatemala, as the result of a classic boarding action. The captain was Don Francisco de Zarate, cousin of the Duke of Medina Sidonia. There was no gold or silver aboard but bales of taffetas and silks, and quantities of 'fine earthern dishes, very finely wrought of fine white earth brought by the Spaniards from the country of China'. (Drake would have been amazed had he known that centuries later China clay produced from his wife's county would be sent from the port of Fowey all over the world.) Zarate was treated so courteously aboard that when he was released he gave Drake a falcon made of gold with an emerald in the beak for a memento of their meeting.

Zarate has left an account of his few days aboard the *Golden Hind*, which is full of interest. Drake asked him if he personally knew the Viceroy of New Spain, Martin Enriquez, and when he answered that he did, the Englishman commented, 'Well, it would give me a greater joy to come across him than all the gold and silver of the Indies.' He could never forget the old score which he had to settle with Enriquez for his treachery to his comrades at San Juan de Ulua. Like the Portuguese da Silva, the Spaniard Zarate had nothing but praise for the *Golden Hind* – in every way she was 'a perfect sailer'. He also envied the way in which Drake exercised his command of the crew, showing that Doughty's execution and the vigorous speeches had had a marked effect on discipline. 'He treats them with affection and they treat him with respect. He carries with him nine or ten cavaliers, cadets of English noblemen. These form part of his council which he calls together for even the most trivial matter, although he takes advice from no one. But he enjoys hearing what they say and afterwards issues his orders. He has no favourites.' Drake punished the least fault.

Those who dined at the Captain's table were served on silver dishes with gold borders; 'he carries all possible dainties and perfumed waters' – many of which were presents from the Queen. 'He dines and sups with viols.' On Sunday, as usual, Drake ordered the ship to be dressed with her flags and banners, while the crew donned their best rig for devotions. Another Spaniard aboard noted the regular reading of the Bible and Chaplain Fletcher's sermons. Zarate also recorded a version of the Doughty affair –

when one of the English gentlemen fervently recommended his captain to return to the Atlantic 'where we are certain of capturing prizes, so that we can give up seeking to make new discoveries', and the man had been put in irons for treachery and later executed. The Spaniard was much alarmed at the beautiful, accurate paintings of the coast which Drake and his nephew had been making, 'for everything is depicted so naturally that anyone who uses these paintings as a guide cannot possibly go astray'.

On the third day, Drake allowed Don Francisco to return to his ship and next day – it was Maundy Thursday – the English raided Guatulco in Guatemala. Twenty men were put in the pinnace as a landing-party to sack the little town, plundering the church of crucifixes and rich ornaments, and entering the town hall where judges were hearing a case against three Negroes who were charged with plotting to burn the settlement; the prisoners were released, two of them joining Drake's crew for a spell. In a conversation with a local merchant, Drake said, 'You will be saying now that this man is a devil, who robs by day and prays by night', yet he was merely obeying his own sovereign's orders and personally regretted taking any property which belonged neither to Prince Philip nor his Viceroy. 'I am not going to stop until I have collected the 2,000,000 crowns that my cousin John Hawkins lost for certain at San Juan de Ulua.' Another Spaniard taken prisoner at Guatulco reported that Drake was proud of being Hawkins's cousin, though he 'is so boastful of himself as a mariner and man of learning that he told him there was no one in the whole world who understood the art [of navigation] better than he'.

Without the slightest warning, on the day he was leaving the Guatemalan coast, Drake dropped the old Portuguese pilot. Nuño da Silva had been his companion for fifteen months and the two had obviously become very close. Some have accused Drake of callously abandoning Nuño to a wretched fate, though he could hardly have known that the man would be taken into custody by the Spaniards and sent to the Viceroy at Mexico City who would, after cross-questioning him about the English corsair's intentions, hand him over to the Inquisition on suspicion of having turned heretic. He was put on the rack, then kept in prison for four years until he was released on Philip II's personal orders. Perhaps Drake's decision to dispense with Nuño's services at that point was taken, in fact, for religious considerations. The *Golden Hind* was now leaving for the north to seek a passage that would, Drake

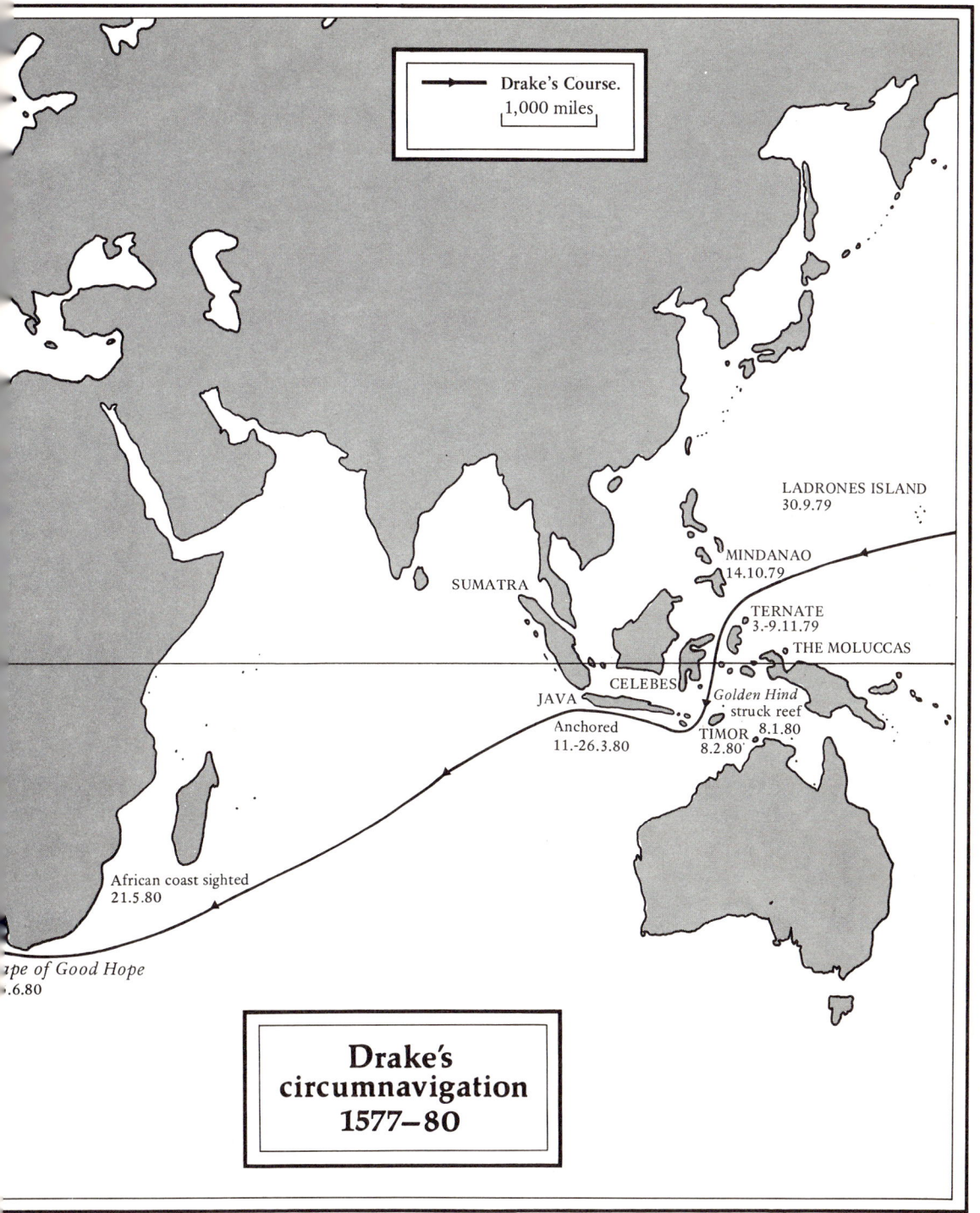

hoped, take him directly home and since there would be no further chance of putting Nuño ashore, he would have to run the not inconsiderable risk of landing in a hostile, Protestant country.

As far as the Spanish could tell, Drake had completely vanished and they diligently searched for him in vain, for the *Golden Hind* was sailing off the west coast of North America. Gradually during their seven-week voyage, the men began to complain of the cold, for it seemed 'the frozen zone, rather than in any way near unto the sun' and there were also days of heavy mist. The map-makers had believed that the coast ran in a north-easterly direction until the 'North-West Passage' were reached, but having reached the latitude of 40°N, near what was to be called Vancouver Island, the English pioneers concluded that there was no such passage, 'or if there be, that yet it is unnavigable'. Though they patiently searched, wrote Francis Fletcher, 'yet we found not the land to trend so much as one point in any place towards the East, but rather running continually North-West, as if it went directly to meet with Africa'. This was a discovery of the first importance. At 48°N, they went about and sailed down the coast to find a suitable haven in a warmer climate and came to anchor in California on 17 June.

The exact location of the anchorage remains uncertain. It cannot have been far from the modern San Francisco and the most likely spot is a bay in the Point Reyes Peninsula, since named 'Drake's Bay'. Because the *Golden Hind* was leaking badly, she was moved near in shore and her valuable cargo was landed so that repairs could be made. The Indians in the district were overjoyed at the arrival of the English party, taking Drake to be a god, and insisting that he become their overlord (or 'Hich'). He named the country New Albion, partly from the white banks and cliffs lying towards the sea, partly because he wanted some affinity with his native land, the Albion of old. Ashore he set up a metal plaque, which read:

> Be it known unto all men by these presents, June 17, 1579, by the Grace of God, in the name of Her Majesty Queen Elizabeth of England and Her successors for ever, I take possession of this Kingdom, whose King and people freely resign their right and title in the whole land unto Her Majesty's keeping, now named by me and to be known unto all men as Nova Albion
>
> Francis Drake

This was six years before Raleigh's Roanoke Colony was established and twenty-eight before the permanent settlement of

Virginia, the earliest of England's North American colonies. They spent five weeks in careening their vessel, caulking the timbers and other repairs and then again put to sea, to the dismay of the Indians. Drake now planned to cross the Pacific Ocean, sailing in the belt of the north-east Trade Winds, to reach the Moluccas.

After two months, they sighted a small group of islands, eight leagues north of the line, but the natives were unfriendly and came out in their canoes to pelt the ship with stones. Drake discharged a single cannon to scare them away. A similar experience in these waters had led Magellan to name an island 'Ladrones' and Drake followed suit by calling this place the 'Isle of Thieves'. Once through the archipelago, they continued on their course and by 21 October were passing by the southern Philippines; the northerly wind prevented the *Golden Hind* from coming close to the land, though a number of canoes, full of warlike natives, came out to investigate the great ship. Thence they came to the group of Spice Islands, or Moluccas, which they reached on 3 November, finding them 'very fruitful and yielding abundance of cloves', of which they purchased six tons very cheaply. The islands were under Portuguese rule, but the colonists were at this time engaged in a fitful war with the Sultan of the neighbouring Malaysian island of Ternate. Coming to that island, the Englishmen were given a warmer welcome. The Sultan made it known that he would like to see the *Golden Hind* at closer range and came out in a canoe to the anchorage. After firing a salvo, accompanied by a fanfare of trumpets, Drake invited him aboard, but the Sultan preferred after all to stay in his canoe. He liked the English music he heard and asked the musicians to come into his boat, to play for him for an hour. During his stay at Ternate, Drake made an agreement with the Sultan by which his people undertook to sell their spices exclusively to English merchants. While Drake was still at the island, a Chinese merchant came to the ship with an interpreter to question him about his voyage and to invite him to visit China before sailing home, but the Captain told him that he was already well behind his schedule. The ship badly needed further careening and a general overhaul, but the English preferred to seek a more isolated spot than Ternate and, after five days, they moved on. Before very long, they arrived at a small uninhabited island, to the south of Celebes, which became their base for four weeks; they called it 'Crab Island', after the large crayfish found there. The blacksmith's forge was set up ashore to assist with repairs and make fresh iron hoops for the water-casks,

The Founding of New Albion

Drake's exploration of the Pacific end of the North-West Passage and his subsequent occupation of the Californian coast have given rise to speculation that it was part of the purpose of the circumnavigation voyage to set up a base for colonial and commercial enterprise in the Pacific. Whatever the motive, Drake insisted on naming the new territory 'New Albion', as a reminder of the old Albion, the homeland from which he had started out.

BELOW Drake in California. In the background, the metal plaque naming New Albion is set up. An illustration from de Bry.

TOP The plaque itself, showing Drake's inscription.

ABOVE Another de Bry entraving: natives at the time of Drake's arrival in New Albion.

while the timbers were recaulked and all the rigging checked. On 12 December 1579, almost two years to the day since leaving Plymouth, they left Crab Island by a westerly course.

Francis Drake had taken the first English ship into the Pacific Ocean, and now he was about to be the first Englishman to enter the Indian Ocean, but he still had to pass through the string of scattered islands and reefs of Indonesia. The lookouts were on the alert for signs of shoaling as Drake searched for a safe passage in these difficult waters and when, after four weeks of tricky navigation, the way ahead seemed at last clear, the sails were fully set to take advantage of a stern wind. Suddenly, on the night of 9 January, the *Golden Hind* went aground on a submerged rock, making an ominous crunching sound, and listed heavily to starboard. The chaplain, Francis Fletcher, led the whole company in prayers and then the pumps were manned. They had tried to put out an anchor to windward, but could not find the sea-bed; with first light they made another attempt, again unsuccessfully, and then began to reduce the weight carried by the ship by casting overboard first the cloves bought at Ternate and then some of their cannon. It was no use; the *Golden Hind* would not move an inch and so the entire crew took the sacrament, most of them convinced that final destruction was only a few hours ahead. There was utter despondency, but Drake himself refused to jettison the richest portions of the cargo and thus admit defeat. And then, after they had been grounded about twenty-four hours, the danger was suddenly over for after the tide had begun to flood, the wind slackened and the vessel began heeling into deep water astern. The *Golden Hind*, which drew thirteen feet of water, had been stuck on a smooth ledge of a submerged reef; to leeward the sounding was only six feet, but to windward the lead could find no bottom. It was a miracle that the planking had escaped serious danger. 'Of all the dangers that in our whole voyage we met with, this was the greatest', wrote the chaplain. This trial was, indeed, far worse than the eeriness of the Doldrums, the fogs of South America, the gale in Magellan's Strait or any of the actions against the Spaniards.

Once they were afloat again and set on a safe course, Drake dealt with his insubordinate chaplain, who had been heard to remark, when they were stranded on the reef, that their fate was divine judgment on the Captain's sin in executing Thomas Doughty. Drake now cleared lower deck and sitting on a sea chest, cross-legged, with a pair of 'pantoufles' in his hand, had Fletcher

OPPOSITE Drake arrives at the Court of the Sultan of Ternate. One of the ships has run aground, and the cannon and spice cargo are being jettisoned. An engraving by Levinius Hulsius.

A detail from a map of Drake's circumnavigation by Nicola van Sype, showing the *Golden Hind* on the rocks off Celebes after the visit to Ternate.

brought before him, with shackles on his feet. 'Francis Fletcher, he solemnly announced, 'I do here excommunicate thee of the Church of God and from all the benefits and graces thereof, and denounce thee to the devil and all his angels.' He was forbidden on pain of death to come before the mast and ordered to wear a placard with the words 'Francis Fletcher, the falsest knave that liveth'. It was a terrifying occasion, as Drake intended it should be. Morale was all important if they were to reach Devon again, and Drake had no time for the faint-hearted whose unspoken thoughts smacked of mutiny; above all, the excommunication was an object lesson in unquestioning obedience to a captain's commands. It was bizarre that a layman should excommunicate an ordained minister of the Church of England, yet Drake was, under his commission, the Queen's personal representative, and in consequence regarded himself as supreme governor in spiritual affairs on his ships no less than Queen Elizabeth herself did in her realm. Fletcher survived his humiliation. The Almighty had, after all, intervened to save them from certain destruction and he acknowledged his fault in giving up hope too easily. A few days afterwards, Drake completely absolved him and reinstated him in his pastoral duties.

They were not yet out of difficulties for, after their terrifying experience in uncharted waters, they proceeded with extreme caution. At length, however, on 12 March they reached Java. Here Drake went ashore and his musicians gave a concert to the Rajah, who later came aboard the *Golden Hind* to return the compliment 'with his own courtly music'. Then they set sail across the Indian Ocean with a fair wind and enjoyed an uneventful passage to make their landfall near modern Durban.

On 15 June they passed the Cape of Good Hope and began the long journey north and west by the African coast. Five weeks later, when they sighted Sierra Leone, they were desperately short of water with no one's ration more than a sixth of a pint; but now, in the mouth of the Tagoine River, they replenished their store of water and refreshed themselves greedily with oysters and lemons. By 15 August they were crossing the Tropic of Cancer and on the 22nd were off the Canaries. The end was almost in sight for the fifty-nine survivors of the original eighty-five men who had left England in the *Pelican*. At last, on 26 September, the *Golden Hind* reached Plymouth, two years, nine months and thirteen days since its departure in December 1577 (after a false start). The men's first question to the fishermen they passed by Prawle Point was if Her Majesty were alive and well, and they loyally responded to the news that she was. They were also told that there was much sickness in Plymouth and so they came to anchor in the Sound, instead of making for a berth alongside. There were few people about to cheer the return of the first Englishman to have encompassed the world – and then Drake realized the reason for his tame welcome. By his careful log it was a Monday, yet in sailing round the globe he had lost a day and so the good people of Plymouth, well enough to be about, were all at church.

5 Corsair Extraordinary

T HE *Golden Hind* CAME TO ANCHOR behind St. Nicholas's Island (as it was still called), in part from uncertainty about the extent of the plague in the town, but also because it was politic to lie quietly until the government's reactions to their depredations were known. Very soon the Mayor of Plymouth was rowed out to welcome the ship and in the Mayor's boat was Mary Drake. It was thirty-two months since husband and wife had seen one another. Often she must have given him up for lost; certainly, after Wynter's return there seemed not a gleam of hope. It was not so much that she was proud of being the wife of a man all Plymouth was saying must be a national hero, but the fact that her Francis had come into harbour safe and sound. For some days Mary stayed aboard, fascinated by his account of their exploits, amazed by the jewels, gold and other treasures. It was hard for her to grasp that she was now a very wealthy woman by any standards.

For his part, Drake listened eagerly to the Mayor to catch up with political news, for there had been great developments during his absence. The most recent news was the most serious. With the death, at the end of August, of Henry the Cardinal, King of Portugal, leaving five claimants to his throne, Philip of Spain, the most obvious candidate, had ordered the Duke of Alva to invade the country and at the battle of Alcántana, near Lisbon, had resoundingly defeated the supporters of Don Antonio, the pretender to the Portuguese crown. It was all over very quickly and as a result Spain had doubled her colonial empire and acquired considerable shipping and harbours in the peninsula. Nearer home, for all the leadership of William the Silent, the Dutch Protestants were losing ground to the Spanish. Don John of Austria had died from a fever, but was succeeded as Spanish commander by the most professional soldier in all Europe, Alexander Farnese, Prince of Parma. Elizabeth herself was fishing in the troubled waters of Netherlands politics and, though no one in Plymouth knew it, was secretly paying subsidies to the doughty Protestant soldier John Casimir from the German Palatinate to aid the Dutch with his mercenaries. Mary Drake would, however, have been full of the Queen's apparent intention to marry the French Prince Francis, Duke of Alençon – a Catholic to boot – who had accepted the title of Defender of Belgic Liberties and was fighting the Spanish in the Southern Netherlands with his eyes on the main chance of carving out a principality for himself. Differences between the southern Catholic region and the northern Calvinist provinces had hardened, and the Union of Utrecht of January 1579 marked the found-

PREVIOUS PAGES Lisbon – a view of the port in 1580.

OPPOSITE Francis Drake at the peak of his extraordinary career, a wealthy man, high in the favour of his Queen.

Habes Lector candide fortiss. ac inuictiss. Ducis Draeck ad viuum Imaginem qui toto terrarum orbe, duorum annorum, et mensium decem spatio, Zephiris fauentibus circumducto, Angliam sedes proprias 4. Cal. Octobr. anno a partu Virginis 1580 reuisit cum antea portu soluisset id. Decem: anni 1577.

ing of a separate Dutch Republic, while the southerners became reconciled to Philip II. Alençon had visited Greenwich to be fêted by Elizabeth, but the proposed marriage negotiations provoked widespread indignation from English Protestants – an attitude Francis Drake now warmly applauded. Maestricht had fallen to the Spanish and now there were Spaniards and Portuguese fighting for the rebel Fitzgerald in Ireland, while in England the Jesuits defied the terrors of the law by their missionary campaign. In France, the Catholic Duke of Guise, a firm supporter of Spain, now carried far more weight than the feeble King Charles IX.

Such was the rather depressing climate which Drake found on his homecoming. And yet he soon learned that there were compensations from his professional point of view. Men in Plymouth talked with admiration about the great strides John Hawkins was making in his new post of Treasurer of the Navy to achieve an unprecedented programme of building men-of-war of a revolutionary design. Drake heard (not, perhaps, without satisfaction) that Frobisher had not succeeded in his quest for a North-West Passage and, alas, that Sir Humphrey Gilbert's expedition to the West Indies the previous year had been a dismal failure. But the Queen, for all her flirtations with a Catholic Prince, was alive and well, Mary, Queen of Scots remained in close captivity and his friends Walsingham and Hatton retained their influence at Court. The fate of his own country, no less than of his own career, would depend primarily on the Queen herself.

On arrival Drake had written to Elizabeth, telling her the main events of his voyage, in which she, as a share-holder, had a strong

The bay of Cascaes, another scene of Drake's naval action against the fleets of Philip II.

personal interest, and making much of the treasure he had captured. Brewer, the trumpeter, took the letter to Court. Already there were rumours that the Queen was 'displeased with him, for that by the way of Peru and Spain she had heard of the robberies he had committed'. He realized – as after Panama – that there might be merit in lying low if policy dictated that the Queen had to bow to criticisms which the corsair knew the Spanish ambassador, Mendoza, must be making about his exploits. He awaited news from Court anxiously. Some of his crew joked that it would be the Tower for him, or a trial in the Admiralty Court. Then the royal message came: Elizabeth would receive him at Court and inspect specimens of the gold and jewellery he had brought home; he had nothing to fear, she assured him. By the same messenger, the Queen sent secretly to Edmund Tremayne, a local Justice of the Peace, to see that the rest of the cargo was safely locked away in Trematon Castle.

Mendoza had demanded an audience of the Queen as soon as he heard of Drake's return, but she had refused to see him until she knew more about Spanish aid to the Irish rebels. For months before the *Golden Hind* returned to Plymouth, the ambassador had been demanding reparation for 'the plunders committed by this vile corsair' and paying spies in western ports to give him news. He heard all about Brewer's ride to London and immediately sent men to Plymouth to find out what they could from members of Drake's crew about the route and the treasure, which he was convinced was being concealed. The haughty Spaniard felt sure that he could use English merchants' fears of reprisals to put pressure on the Queen to restore the booty, or at least to come to terms, but it was galling to have to write to Philip, his master, that he was so weak at sea that Englishmen could 'offend you with impunity'. He felt that he was cutting a ridiculous figure, with Drake's success infecting everyone. Soon Drake was boasting that he had plans for returning to the Americas with six ships, offering his shareholders a return of seven hundred per cent. 'This has so great an influence over Englishmen that everybody wants to have a share in the expedition.'

It was Drake, not Mendoza, who spent six hours at Richmond Palace closeted with the Queen while she questioned him, fascinated by his relation of the hazardous voyage as he pointed to the map he had brought, and overjoyed at the gold ducats and other specimens he offered. The two of them got on famously, though this was only the third time he had seen Elizabeth to talk to; she called him her 'pirate' and liked his Devonian speech, which was almost the same as that of her new favourite, Walter Raleigh. Soon Drake was riding back to Plymouth to make a full inventory of the treasure. She let him keep £10,000 for himself and share a similar sum among his crew, but the rest was to be placed for greater safety in the Tower of London, until grave decisions had been taken. In the end, despite wavering by some councillors, nothing was returned to Spain and the investors received a return on their money of 4,700 per cent! No wonder Drake was a hero at Court and in the city, no less than in the ports. The Queen's pickings, which she so badly needed to reduce the drain on her purse of the leaping costs of administration and defence, were probably not less than £300,000, for we know that besides her return on her shares she also took an independent 'bounty'. But for this reserve of 'chested treasure' in the Tower, her subjects would have had to have borne a far more pinching rate of direct taxation throughout the long naval war with Spain that dominated the last eighteen years of her reign. But there was rather more to it than this. The economist J. M. Keynes used to regard the Queen's share of the booty brought home in the *Golden Hind* as the 'origins of British Foreign Investment', for out of her proceeds Elizabeth made a very substantial investment in the new Levant Company trading to the Eastern Mediterranean. 'Largely out of the profits of the Levant Company', wrote Keynes, 'there was financed the East India Company, the profits of which during the seventeenth and eighteenth centuries were the main foundation of England's foreign connections; and so on.'

Francis Drake was now an international figure, as well as 'all England's hero'. William the Silent wondered if a medal was being struck in honour of his exploit; the King of Denmark wanted to name his finest warship after him; King Henry of Navarre asked if he could acquire copies of his charts, superimposed with the route he had taken; even the Catholic Duke of Florence enquired if he could obtain a true likeness of the great man for hanging in his portrait gallery. At home he was mobbed in London and became overnight the hero of the ballad-makers' verses which were sold as broad-sheets at street corners. Anglican divines and Puritan ministers referred in their sermons to his exploits against the Spanish in terms of David slaying Goliath or Moses defeating Pharaoh's army; grammar school boys were set the task of penning Latin hexameters about his triumphs and Court versifiers sang his praises:

> Let Captains crouch and cowards leave to crake
> And give the fame to little Captain Drake.

He had caught the public imagination. England had badly needed a hero and now one had emerged deserving every ounce of the pent-up adulation that was voiced. His success story had all the ingredients of a first-class drama and the Devonian had not only proved himself an intrepid fighter and brilliant explorer, but had won untold riches. 'The people generally applauded his wonderful adventures and rich prizes', wrote John Stow. 'His name and fame became admirable in all places, the people swarming daily in the streets to behold him, swearing hatred to all that misliked him.' And at Court his star was dominant. Mendoza, thoroughly put out, told Philip II that 'he passes much time with the Queen, by whom he is highly favoured and told how great is the service he has rendered her'. He had presented her with a crown encrusted with five emeralds, 'three of them almost as long as a little finger, and two round ones'. She wore it on New Year's Day, when Drake gave her a further present of a diamond cross valued at five thousand crowns. 'She says she will knight him on the day she goes to see his ship, which she has ordered to be brought ashore and placed' at Deptford 'as a curiosity', reported the crestfallen ambassador.

Before the crew was paid off, the *Golden Hind* was sailed on a triumphant final voyage, like the last lap of a *victor ludorum*, from Plymouth round to Deptford, to berth near the building of the Trinity House pilots. Here came the Queen with a great entourage on 4 April. Not long before she arrived, there had been an accident, when the wooden bridge constructed for her to pass over the muddy ways collapsed under the weight of sightseers, though no one was injured. Aboard, a banquet had been prepared. As Elizabeth was boarding the vessel, one of her purple and gold garters slipped down and the Seigneur de Marchamont, personal agent in London of the Duke of Alençon, claimed it as his lawful prize for sending to his lovesick master, but the Queen demanded it back 'as she had nothing else with which to keep her stocking up', promising that she would surrender it again on returning to Greenwich Palace. Everyone was in high spirits, though Drake's investiture was to be much more than a domestic event, for Elizabeth intended to make as much political capital out of it as she could. She slyly told the kneeling corsair that she had ready a gilded sword to strike off his head for turning pirate, and then she

The silver cup given to Drake by Elizabeth to encase the coconut which he had brought back for her after the circumnavigation.

Elizabeth knights Drake at Deptford in 1581: from a bronze in the Prince's Chamber at the House of Lords.

handed the sword to de Marchamont, asking him to perform the ceremony for her. This, indeed, foreshadowed an Anglo-French league against Spain. In view of the impending arrival in England of a great French delegation to hammer out the terms of a marriage treaty between Elizabeth and Alençon (whom she nicknamed her 'Frog'), Drake's present to the Queen of a frog encrusted with diamonds was in a pawkish vein of humour. Elizabeth asked to be introduced to Drake's wife, Mary, and then insisted on seeing over the entire ship. Her gifts to him on this occasion were a beautiful pendant jewel, enclosing her portrait in a miniature of Nicholas Hilliard, and a scarf of green silk, bordered with gold lace and embroidery at both ends of which a motto was worked in fine gold thread: *'The Almighty be your Guide and your Protector to the End.'* Mendoza (the only member of the diplomatic corps not to be invited to Deptford) was aghast. In his view, Drake was a pirate who deserved to be severely punished, probably executed, and now his sovereign had knighted him and blasphemously given him a holy text to preserve his life. War between England and Spain was inevitable.

A greater royal gift was to follow. Letters patent were issued stating that 'Whereas Sir Francis Drake, Knight, has circumnavigated the globe from east to west and has discovered in the south part of the world many unknown places, Her Majesty to perpetuate his fame and valour doth grant unto him and his heirs' the manor of Sherford in Devon and smaller properties in the Midlands and North Country. At the time, Sherford was leased to his kinsman Thomas Maynard, who continued to reside there. The following New Year's Day, the Queen gave him a goblet of silver engraved with a representation of his ship which had made history. The vessel itself was to be laid up at Deptford, near to the spot at which he had been knighted. Here a special dock was constructed and for three generations sightseers came to marvel at the tiny craft and pay homage to the memory of the man who had sailed her (in his turn came Samuel Pepys, Secretary of the Admiralty under Charles II) but later the famous exhibit became neglected; souvenir hunters chipped away at the timber and eventually the sarcophagus was empty. Two pieces of furniture made from the timbers survive – a table in the Inner Temple and a chair in the Bodleian Library, Oxford.

A knight required a county seat and Drake could certainly afford to pay a substantial price for his. He did not have far to look, for Buckland Abbey, which belonged to Richard Grenville, in his own county, so near to his native Tavistock, was on the market. The Cistercian Abbey had been founded by the Countess of Devon in 1278 and had passed soon after the Dissolution to Sir Richard

Drake's seal, showing his coat of arms and, at the top, the *Golden Hind*.

Grenville of Bideford, whose grandson, the seaman, inherited the property in 1550. During his thirty years' occupation, he made great changes, converting the old abbey church into his hall, and building offices and store rooms in the cloisters. Over the great fireplace in the hall, he had placed four classical figures in plaster work, representing the virtues Justice, Temperance, Patience and Fortitude. Outside were the remains of the monastery gardens and further afield a pleasant park, well stocked with deer. Drake showed great astuteness over his negotiations, for he sensed that Grenville regarded him as an upstart and would never knowingly agree to let him acquire the house, so at the beginning of 1581 he used his friends Christopher Harris and John Hele to buy the Buckland estate in their own names for the considerable sum of £3,400, and in the autumn they conveyed it to Sir Francis. Land was the fundamental wealth of Tudor England and the corsair in using his prize money to invest in a landed estate was only copying the regular practice of successful merchants. He had become a country gentleman and, perhaps, would found a county family.

Just before he and Mary moved in to Buckland, he had been elected Mayor of Plymouth for the first time. This was an honour which meant much to him; he took his duties seriously and had perforce, to reside much of the year at his house in Plymouth. During the period of his office, he began the scheme for bringing a fresh water supply to the town, which took ten years to complete, and also set up a compass on the Hoe, 'to guide mariners to the fabled west'. Mayor Drake entertained the envoy of the Portuguese Pretender, Don Antonio, who had escaped after the battle of Alcántana to the Azores and managed to retain the islands' allegiance. A scheme was prepared for Drake to sail to the Azores and with Don Antonio's support use them as a base for attacking the Spanish Plate Fleet. Walsingham was vigorously supporting this plan which he was convinced must be followed in conjunction with France, but somehow it became swamped by more pressing diplomatic problems.

While Sir Francis chafed at having to be ashore, his wife was thankful that they remained together for the longest period since their marriage. Yet Mary was not long to enjoy the status of Lady Drake and the added distinction of being mistress of Buckland and Mayoress of Plymouth. She died in January 1583 and was buried in the chapel of St Budeaux, by the Tamar, where they had been married not quite fourteen years previously.

Drake was possibly not by her side at Buckland when she died,

The Knight Acquires a County Seat

Drake returned from his circumnavigation of the world a millionaire by modern standards, an international figure and the national hero of the day, knighted by his Queen. It was fitting, therefore, that he should have a home worthy of his newly won glory and, after some secret negotiations on his behalf by two friends with the owner Richard Grenville, he acquired the estate of Buckland Abbey, originally in the possession of the Cistercian order.

LEFT The tree-shaded exterior of Buckland Abbey, in Drake's home county of Devon.

ABOVE Drake's panelled dining room, hung with portraits of Queen Elizabeth and Sir John Hawkins, and filled with richly carved furniture.
LEFT A fireplace in Buckland Abbey, with Drake's coat of arms built in above the mantelpiece.

for we know that he had been to Court for the New Year to present a customary offering to the Queen, a reminder that he still lacked employment afloat. On this occasion it was a splendid gold salt-cellar, shaped like a globe, supported by two naked men, 'being the history of Jupiter and Pallas, with a woman on the top thereof, with a trumpet in her hand – the foot enamelled with flowers'. His New Year's gifts to Her Majesty were always unusual as well as extravagant; perhaps the one which she treasured most was his gift in 1587 of a fan of red and white feathers, splendidly jewelled, which opened to show her own portrait.

One distressing epilogue to the circumnavigation was the legal action brought against Drake by John Doughty, who prosecuted him in the Earl Marshal's court for murdering his brother in Patagonia. Sir Francis contended that such a case lay outside the jurisdiction of the Marshal and he applied for a writ from the Court of Queen's Bench to stay the proceedings. The Lord Chief Justice earned some unpopularity by ruling that Doughty was entitled to proceed and it cannot have been pleasant for Sir Francis to have the case hanging over his head, but there, in fact, the matter rested, for Drake never went for trial as young Doughty was found to be involved in underhand dealings with the Spanish. Realizing that there was now no chance of restitution from the English government, a group of Spanish merchants attempted to come to terms with Drake himself and their agent in England, Pedro de Zubiaur, struck up a friendship with John Doughty. It came out that when chances of negotiating with Sir Francis for a return of part of his plunder proved hopeless, there was a plot to murder him. Doughty had written a letter which ran 'when the Queen did Knight Drake she did then Knight the arrantest Knave, the vilest villain, the falsest thief and the cruelest murderer that ever was born'; and then a servant of Hatton's reported that he had heard Doughty swear that he would kill him. Such threats were common form in Elizabethan England, but Doughty and another English contact of de Zubiaur were arrested and on the rack revealed that Philip II had offered a reward of twenty thousand ducats to anyone who would either kidnap Drake and send him to Spain, or bring his head to the Escorial on a charger. Doughty was prepared to make the attempt himself. For all his boasted connections with Lord Burghley, he failed to gain release from his cell in the Marshalsea Prison.

Despite the exploits of Drake and others to humble Spanish maritime power, the Protestant cause in Europe was sinking, and at home the Queen was in great danger. These were the days of plots and counter-plots, of Walsingham's espionage system at its height, of the tracking down of seminary priests who preached treason and tyrannicide and of the patient cracking of ciphers. The discovery of the Throckmorton plot to assassinate Elizabeth hastened the expulsion of Mendoza from England at the opening of 1584, for conspiring with Mary, Queen of Scots and the House of Guise. He was the last Spanish ambassador to England during the reign, and his parting shot was 'As I have apparently failed to please the Queen as a minister of peace, she would in future force me to try to satisfy her in war.' Open war with Spain, indeed, seemed inevitable. The death of Alençon from a fever at Midsummer brought the House of Guise to consolidate the various Catholic factions in France into a league to oppose the Protestant Henry of Navarre, the new heir to the throne, and soon there was a firm Paris–Madrid axis. In the Netherlands, Parma went from strength to strength, capturing the chief cities of the south, but worse was to come, for in July William the Silent was assassinated.

In this crisis, Elizabeth decided to summon a new Parliament and for the first time Drake sat in the House of Commons to which he was returned as member for Bossiney, near Tintagel, in north Cornwall. Though 'party' labels are inapposite, he supported the faction which looked to Francis Walsingham as leader, anxious to have the fleet in full readiness for war, even if this meant crippling taxes; at home to hound the Jesuits and seminary priests to death by new, draconian legislation, and also to make it impossible for Mary, Queen of Scots to succeed to the throne of England, even if – dreadful thought – her supporters succeeded in murdering Elizabeth as even the Prince of Orange had been murdered. In London before the sessions opened, Drake was called to the Privy Council for discussions on naval policy and on the day before the opening of Parliament he was named as leading member of a syndicate undertaking 'the charge of the Navy to the Moluccas'. The sum of £40,000 was being put up by the Queen, Leicester, the Hawkins family, Raleigh, Hatton and himself to equip a fleet to go to the Spice Islands, not as a trading venture but as a military operation. This was a plan which clearly stemmed from Drake's visit to the Moluccas on his voyage round the world and was intended as a blow at a rich corner of the old Portuguese Empire that was far from the main centres of Spanish colonial power. The preparations went forward throughout the resumed Parliamentary session of the early spring of 1585, but before Drake's fleet was

ready to sail, the political situation had changed and he was, instead, ordered to the West Indies.

In February 1585 Sir Francis married again. This time his bride was not an unknown country lass, like Mary Newman, but an heiress from a well-established Somerset family. Elizabeth, the only child of Sir George Sydenham of Combe Sydenham, was then about twenty – just under half Drake's age – and a great beauty, taller than her spouse and with delicate hands. A millionaire by modern standards, the widower was the best match in England and no doubt could have had the pick of many daughters from noble households, yet he chose to court Mistress Sydenham, who was related to an old family friend from Tavistock, John Fitz. The marriage settlement between Drake and Elizabeth's father records the landed property which the former had acquired since purchasing Buckland.

Despite marrying a new wife, he was soon keen to be afloat again. He was convinced that the surest way of crippling Philip II would be to cut off his supply of gold and silver from the Indies, but Elizabeth was cautious, not wanting to endorse a strategical plan which might cost her money. The last year or so had seen great activity by other seamen, spurred on by Drake's own success, and further plans for exploration, colonization and conquest in distant parts. Ralph Fitch and John Eldred, two merchants, had left in 1583 on expeditions which took them to Mesopotamia, the Persian Gulf and India; John Davis was setting out for another search for the North-West Passage and on his voyage would visit Greenland and later discover Davis Strait. Then, in April 1585, as the culmination of years of discussion, argument and planning by Sir Humphrey Gilbert, now dead, the Hakluyts, Sir Richard Grenville and the Queen's favourite from Devonshire, Walter Raleigh, an expedition left England to plant England's first settlement in North America. Elizabeth had refused to allow Raleigh leave from Court to head the expedition but she let him call his colony at Roanoke 'Virginia', after her. Grenville had sailed with seven ships and about a hundred settlers under Ralph Lane, who was appointed governor.

Before Grenville's ships had reached North America, Philip II ordered the arrest of all English merchant ships in Spanish and Portuguese ports, as a reprisal for the English corsairs' depredations across the Line. This was taken in England as a declaration of war, and so instead of striking at the Moluccas, Drake's fleet was first to rescue English merchants stranded in the Peninsula and

OPPOSITE Elizabeth Sydenham, Lady Drake, the beautiful second wife of one of the most eligible gentlemen in the land.

then to aim for the West Indies, where the Admiral's expertise was indisputable. Twenty-nine warships were ready, the largest being the *Elizabeth Bonaventure* of six hundred tons in which Drake flew his flag. Martin Frobisher was Vice-Admiral and among the captains were Richard Hawkins (John's son), Edmund Wynter (a son of Sir William), Drake's youngest brother, Thomas, Leicester's brother-in-law, Francis Knollys, a grandson of Burghley's, William Cecil, and a West Countryman, Thomas Fenner, whom Drake highly regarded; Fenner was to work closely with him in the 1588 campaign. This was to be a military as much as a naval operation, for there were twelve companies of soldiers – about 2,300 men – under the command of Christopher Carleill, Walsingham's son-in-law. A disgruntled Sir Philip Sidney had escaped from Court to join Drake at Plymouth, but the Admiral feared the Queen's fury when she learned that he had joined the fleet and warned her of his plans, so that messengers came with orders for his return. In any case, Drake had no room aboard for an inexperienced sailor whose sole idea of the expedition was that England should seize and hold a base in the New World.

At last, on 14 September 1585, Drake's fleet sailed and made for Vigo Bay. In case the Queen should change her mind and summon him to London, as she had summoned Sidney, he did not wait to complete the victualling of his ships once his sailing-orders arrived. He landed parties at Vigo and Bayona in search of booty and to evacuate any English merchants, but all of them chose to stay, unaware that an irrevocable breach in relations with Spain was taking place, as they had their accounts to settle; for them business was business, for Drake there could be nothing but action. He left the Spanish coast with colours flying, triumphant, and no Spanish man-of-war was sent to pursue him. 'If the influence of sea-power on history is what has been claimed for it,' wrote Sir Julian Corbett seventy-five years ago, 'then this moment marks an epoch.' Drake had cocked a snook at Spain and was off to the West Indies, the next objective.

He had planned to sack San Domingo, La Hacha and Santa Marta in turn, rendering them defenceless, and then to take Cartagena. Afterwards he would deal with Nombre de Dios and Panama, both for Drake of famous memory, and perhaps raid Havana. This was a grandiose scheme and in the event a number of factors prevented the Spanish Colonial Empire from being crippled on such a scale. The fleet's first halt was at the Canaries, which would provide useful provisions, yet the weather was too rough to make

OPPOSITE Sir Walter Raleigh he founded the first ill-fated Roanoke colony in Virginia six years after Drake set up his plaque in New Albion. Virginia later became the first of the English colonies in North America.

A map of all the Americas, as known to sailors at the end of the sixteenth century, from de Bry's *Americæ Pars Sexta* (1596). The figures of Columbus, Magellan, Florentinus and Pisard with maps and nautical instruments surround the map.

a landing at Las Palmas. Drake then made for the Cape Verde Islands – somewhat off his main route – where he sacked the towns of Santiago and Porto Praya, but then, after a promising beginning, things began to go wrong, for a violent fever took a heavy toll of his men; some three hundred of them died and a great many more were to remain seriously ill for the rest of the expedition. By the middle of December, they were in the Antilles and at St Christopher thoroughly cleansed the ships and prepared the soldiers for campaigning. Drake had sent a party to reconnoitre San Domingo, the capital of Hispaniola and the administrative hub of the Caribbean. He learned that though it was heavily defended, there was a beach suitable for landing men ten miles west of the port and on 1 January 1586 he put ashore Carleill and his soldiers, while the fleet made a show of force off the town.

It was all soon over, for the Spaniards had been completely surprised. Great quantities of guns and ammunition were captured, but no treasure could be found, so Drake opened negotiations with the inhabitants for a ransom to be paid, to save them from a holocaust. After the ceasefire, there was a strange contrast in the relations between victors and vanquished, veering from old-world courtesy to wanton brutality. Under the flag of truce, a Spaniard had killed a Negro servant belonging to Sir Francis, who felt provoked into hanging two friars and cursing that he would hang all prisoners in his hands unless the culprit was surrendered. The man was duly produced and ordered to be hanged by his fellows. While haggling over the ransom money, for which he had to reduce his demands to 25,000 ducats, Drake teased some of the Spaniards by asking them to translate a Latin inscription carved on a staircase over Philip II's royal arms. The words were '*Non sufficit orbis*' ('This world is not big enough for him').

After a month, the men re-embarked and made for Cartagena, a much more impregnable bastion. The fleet anchored in the lagoon and when darkness came, the troops were landed on the peninsula to approach the seaward defences of the city in dead ground, safe from enemy fire. It was Drake's own plan which Carleill so effectively carried out and, as at San Domingo, after a brief clash of arms the place surrendered, for the governor was at a complete loss to understand how he had been outwitted by so small and inexperienced a band of warriors. The English stayed at Cartagena for seven weeks, during which fever was again rampant and any thoughts Drake might have had about holding the stronghold with an English garrison had to be abandoned, so the batteries were

OPPOSITE Sir Richard Grenville, another of Drake's rivals in maritime enterprise. He commanded the *Revenge* on its final tragic voyage in 1592.

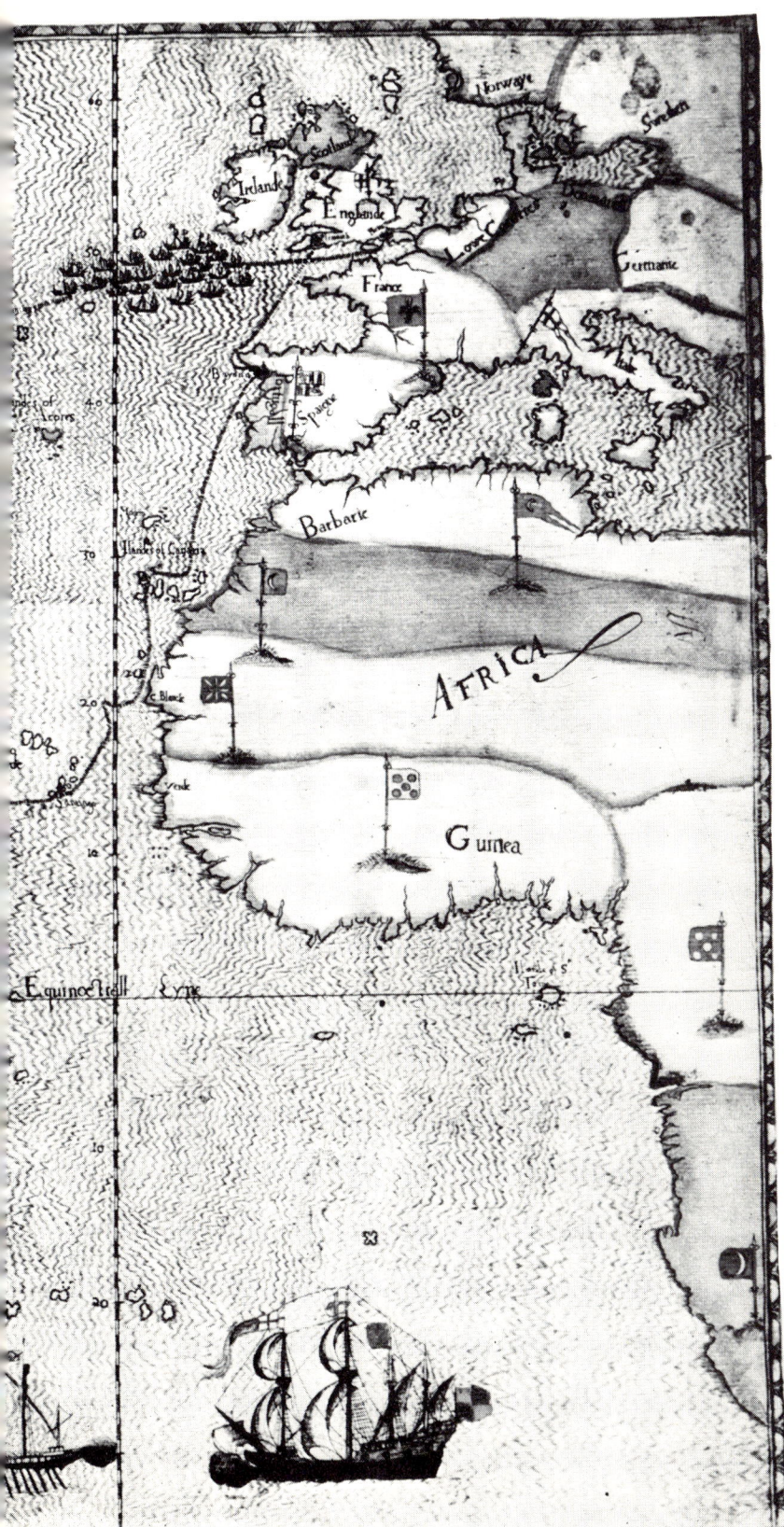

A map illustrating the route taken by Drake on his Caribbean voyage of 1585–6 (from Boazzio's engravings).

Boazzio's view of Drake's fleet in action, ready to take Saint Augustine.

stripped of their guns and the other defences rendered useless. Once again, no significant amount of treasure was found and the terms of the ransom were finally settled at the modest payment of 110,000 ducats, though this did not include a sum for the fort, which Drake thereupon demolished. With so many men still on the sick list, the dream of raiding Panama from across the Isthmus completely faded, so Drake decided to make for home, bearing off sixty captured guns, bells and metal and the more valuable contents of merchants' dwellings. He also took with him Negroes and liberated galley slaves. His plan was to return by way of Cuba and Florida, taking such prizes as he should meet with and he never ruled out the chance of intercepting the Mexican Plate Fleet. Perhaps, as he reported to Burghley on his return, he had missed the Plate Fleet by a mere twelve hours, because 'we had in that instant very foul weather'. If so, this was a great blow to the enterprise, but it seems that Drake was possibly referring to his operations the previous autumn off the peninsula.

There is an interesting glimpse of the Admiral in the thick of the heavy work, when the fleet was at Cape Antonio, with many of the men still suffering from the effects of fever. 'To encourage others and to hasten the getting of fresh water about the ships [he] took no less pains himself than the meanest; as also at San Domingo, Cartagena and other places . . . with such wonderful travail of body as doubtless had he been the meanest person, as he was the chiefest', wrote Captain Biggs. Now he devastated the settlement of Saint Augustine on the coast of Florida, where the Spaniards had succeeded the first French Huguenot colonists, removing the great guns and taking off a chest or more of money.

His last port of call was the infant colony of Virginia, which he reached on 9 June. The main fleet anchored outside while Drake went ashore to meet Ralph Lane who had been facing serious difficulties since Grenville's departure the previous August. The Admiral offered to transport all the settlers home, but if they wanted to stay, he would allot them a suitable vessel and as many provisions as he could spare. Lane decided to remain and so a ship was left with a considerable quantity of stores. That night, however, a violent storm arose and the vessel assigned to Lane was cast away. For three days, the howling gale persisted and certain ships of the fleet were in great danger from the perilous anchorage. Lane's courage and confidence were badly sapped and, as a result, he decided to embark his settlers for a return to England with Drake. So ended Raleigh's first Roanoke colony, since the fifteen persons who chose to remain in Virginia were never heard of again. As luck would have it, a fortnight after they had sailed, Grenville returned to Roanoke with three stout ships and ample supplies, but Drake cannot – any more than Lane – be blamed for making what was under the circumstances a sensible decision.

On 28 July 1586 Drake reached Plymouth, having inflicted a terrible wound on the Spanish Empire. His operations at San Domingo and Cartagena had shown how vulnerable the strongholds of the Spanish Main were to a corsair extraordinary, and they ruined Philip II's credit with the banking houses of Europe. Not only was Parma in the Netherlands short of money for his troops who were fighting the Dutch, but the merchants of Old Spain were feeling the pinch. Englishmen at large began to realize that the tide had begun to turn, for if England was very far from being out of danger, her enemy was certainly no longer 'invincible' by land and sea.

6 Singeing the King of Spain's Beard

'TRULY, SIR FRANCIS DRAKE is a fearful man to the King of Spain', wrote Lord Burghley on his triumphant return from the West Indies; and yet the Admiral's exploits in the following year, when he was at the peak of his prowess and daring, were to humble Philip II even more remarkably, so that euphemistically it was said that he singed the King's beard. In the ten months during which he had been away in the New World, the political landscape at home had darkened. Open war with Spain became daily nearer. Under the Treaty of Nonsuch, Elizabeth had committed herself to sending 1,000 horse and 5,100 foot soldiers to fight for the Dutch Republic's survival, and the campaign had gone badly, since the Prince of Parma had followed up his sack of Antwerp with the capture of Venloo.

In Madrid, Brussels and Rome, plans for a Spanish Enterprise against England went forward. The Spanish Admiral, the Marquis of Santa Cruz, had a few years previously proposed that a combined naval and military expedition should be mounted against heretic England, but Philip II had at first considered it too costly an undertaking; but now that England had openly intervened in the Netherlands to support his rebellious subjects, he decided that he could no longer postpone an attack on Elizabeth's realm and would draft from the campaign in the Netherlands as many troops as could be spared to cross the Channel under Parma while a great fleet controlled the Narrow Seas. All the reports which Philip meticulously conned in his study in the Escorial left him in no doubt that it was his plain Christian duty to invade England, depose Elizabeth and restore the Catholic faith. 'God is my witness', he wrote to the Cortes, 'that it is not the desire to gain new kingdoms that guided me, but the zeal for his service and the hope of glorifying the Holy faith. For this I have risked everything.' Pope Sixtus V, who had long been urging vigorous action from the greatest of the Catholic powers to implement Pius V's bull of 1570, which deposed Elizabeth, blessed the Enterprise as a Crusade of the Church, though he was wary about subscribing funds. First reports of the Spanish preparations reached London in December 1585, but it was not until the very eve of Drake's return from the West Indies that the Queen began to take the threat at all seriously, by ordering the lords lieutenant in the shires to muster the militia and arrange for a system of beacons to signal the approach of a hostile fleet. Almost until the Armada was in the Channel, Elizabeth pinned her faith on avoiding direct conflict by discreet negotiation.

PREVIOUS PAGES A view of Cadiz, showing the main features of the seaport.

OPPOSITE Drake, whose naval strategy was paramount in weakening the strength of Philip II's Catholic sea forces.

FRANCIS
DRAECK

The third recent political development, and the most serious, was the implication of the captive Mary, Queen of Scots in the Babington Plot to murder Elizabeth, which Sir Francis Walsingham succeeded in unravelling as Drake landed at Portsmouth. The conspirators, unaware that Philip's Enterprise against England was being pressed forward vigorously, were expecting Parma to support their design from the troops under his command. Mary's trial and subsequent execution the following February, after Elizabeth had overcome her reluctance to sign the warrant condemning her royal cousin to death, intensified Spanish efforts, for before the end Mary had recognized Philip II as her heir to both the English and the Scottish thrones. Francis Drake had readily signed the Bond of Association to come to the defence of Elizabeth and avenge her death, should such a disaster occur, but he did not seek election to the Parliament summoned in October 1586 with but one item of government business to be discussed – the fate of the Queen of Scots – though Puritan friends tried unsuccessfully to embark on a root and branch reform of the Church of England. As a man of action, he was itching to be at sea again, fighting the Spaniards in their own waters, and would have found Parliamentary affairs burdensome. 'There is now a very great gap opened, very little to the liking of the King of Spain', he had written as open war loomed nearer daily. 'God work it all to His Glory.'

Drake looked to the Dutch, Protestants like himself, whose earliest stand against Spanish tyranny had been fathered by fellow corsairs – the 'Beggars of the Sea' – operating under William the Silent's letters of marque since July 1569. Leicester, a fervent supporter of Drake at Court, was now Lieutenant-General of the English army in the Northern Netherlands, even though the Queen had thwarted his ambition of becoming Governor of those Provinces. Sir Francis cherished a scheme which would extend the Treaty of Nonsuch between England and the States General by enabling the navies, as well as the armies, of the two countries to take part in joint operations against Spain. Such would provide England with additional shipping which she badly needed. Drake came over to Holland early in October with eight ships, bringing Leicester further troops and supplies, and was accorded a grand reception by the Dutch, yet the Estates General would not give him the support he wanted until his Queen had assumed the sovereignty of the Netherlands – a political role she had made clear she would never fill. He did, however, have useful discussions with merchants in the ports who readily expressed an interest in taking

OPPOSITE The Marquis of Santa Cruz, whose idea it originally was to plan a joint naval and military attack on Philip's heretic enemy.

out shares in a further West Indies venture. Next month he returned to England, bringing home Leicester, who had put his army into winter quarters. By then the position of Mary, Queen of Scots was being hotly discussed on all sides. Drake wasted no time in applying to the Privy Council for a licence to put to sea, but it was refused him. What he was contemplating was a further raid on the Spanish Main, but the government wanted him nearer to hand. The Queen and others were frightened of leaving the defence of the English Channel by the navy's 'wooden walls' at anything below maximum strength, for the latest reports from Spain suggested that Philip's preparations for an invasion had reached an advanced stage and there was also anxiety lest the ruling House of Guise in France should attempt to intervene by force on behalf of Mary. Although there was still no formal declaration of war against Spain, Elizabeth's chances of negotiation to avoid open war became daily more remote. One plan, for a squadron to sail to the Spanish coast to reconnoitre and make an impressive display of England's sea power, was abandoned for fear that the Armada might succeed in entering the Channel while the fleet was at reduced strength. Yet with the coming of winter, England was out of immediate danger and at Christmas it was decided that the entire fleet should be mobilized by three months hence 'to impeach the provisions of Spain'. The strategical plan adopted and the name of the commander were kept close secrets until the beginning of March 1587 when at last it became known that Drake was going to sea again.

Sir Francis was now busy at Plymouth preparing the squadron which had been placed under his command. At the core of this fleet of twenty-three ships were four of the Queen's men-of-war – the *Elizabeth Bonaventure*, in which Drake again flew his flag; the *Golden Lion*, commanded by William Borough, Clerk of the Queen's ships, a man immensely knowledgeable about naval affairs but relatively inexperienced afloat, who was appointed Vice-Admiral for the expedition; the *Dreadnought* sailing under Drake's old friend Thomas Fenner, and the *Rainbow*, a fast new galleon, making its maiden voyage. Her Majesty also lent two pinnaces. Lord Admiral Howard furnished a war ship and a pinnace, while the Levant Company, whose traffic with Crete and the eastern Mediterranean remained in grave danger so long as Spanish sea power was unchecked, provided seven large vessels under Robert Flick, the Rear-Admiral. Drake himself subscribed four ships, the largest being the *Thomas*, a privateer of two hundred tons. To

OPPOSITE Charles Howard, Baron Effingham and Lord High Admiral: he provided a war ship and a pinnace for the campaign against Philip.

The *Golden Lion*, typical of the English ships that engaged in combat with the Armada – smaller than the Spanish ones, they were, however, far more seaworthy.

finance the operations, a special syndicate was formed and each shareholder expected to receive a rich return on his money. The object of the expedition was 'to prevent or withstand such enterprises as might be attempted against Her Highness's realm or dominions', especially by hampering Philip's admirals from concentrating in one port the squadrons being made ready in different harbours for the Enterprise against England. If the Armada was already on its way to northern waters, Drake was to go into the attack and then cut off its supplies. He was also under orders to capture the trading fleets returning from both the West and the East Indies. Finally, he was empowered, as he had specifically requested, 'to distress the ships within the havens themselves'.

These comprehensive sailing orders were all that Drake desired, yet Queen and Council had second thoughts. If Philip II were not provoked too far, he might still be prepared to negotiate a peace, and so the commander's freedom of action was at the last minute greatly curbed; the expedition was now envisaged by the Queen as an essay in gun-boat diplomacy, rather than a full-blooded naval campaign. A messenger rode down to Plymouth with revised orders: 'You shall forbear to enter forcibly into any of the King's ports or havens, or to offer any violence to any of his towns or shipping . . . or to do any act of hostility upon the land.' In short, the expedition was now to be a cruise, with the vessels undertaking warlike acts only outside territorial waters. Experience had taught Drake that the Queen might well change her mind and so, the day after the Levant Company ships came into the Sound, he weighed anchor, eager to be gone, for the weather was fair. Before leaving Plymouth, he sent Walsingham a letter which breathes his unexampled excitement for action, ever confident in the outcome: 'The winds command me away. Our ship is under sail. God grant we may live in His fear as the enemy may have cause to say that God doth fight for Her Majesty as well abroad as at home' – a reference to Mary's execution and the rounding up of Jesuit priests. 'Pray unto God for us that He will direct us in the right way; then we shall not doubt our enemies, for they are the sons of men.'

Altogether there were 2,200 men serving in the twenty-three sail, and they formed the strongest force Queen Elizabeth had as yet sent to sea. The fleet was a distant sight of masts on the horizon by the time the Council's messenger came to the Hoe. A natural son of John Hawkins was sent out with the despatch in a fast

OPPOSITE A portrait of Lord Howard of Effingham by Cockson. As Lord Admiral he was titular commander-in-chief of the operations against the Armada.

An engraving showing the entrance to Cadiz Harbour, massed with ships.

pinnace but by a happy device he failed to deliver it to Drake, making the excuse that a sudden gale had made it impossible for him to reach the *Elizabeth Bonaventure*. When the news of Drake's subsequent triumphs came to the Queen's ears, she must have been supremely thankful that her countermanding orders had been sent too late.

On 5 April, three days from port, Drake was in sight of Cape Finisterre, then a gale scattered his ships and they did not resume their stations in company until the 16th, when they were off Lisbon, the port in which Santa Cruz was assembling his Armada. Rather than attack Lisbon, Drake decided to sail on with his fastest ships to Cadiz where, he understood, there were many other galleons. Three days later, he was ready to attack the port. He called Borough, the Vice-Admiral, and the other captains to the *Elizabeth Bonaventure* to give them their instructions, but deliberately refused to let them consider his proposal as a formal council of war, which was the convention. Borough, a Navy Board man and a stickler for precedent and tradition, registered his protest. The Vice-Admiral considered it the height of rashness for Drake to sail into Cadiz harbour, and said so. There was much to be said for Borough's caution; the harbour was well protected by natural features and the one safe channel passed dangerously close to the shore batteries. No one knew the exact state of the port's defences. At least, counselled Borough, wait until dark and act according to the conventions of naval warfare by sending a proper challenge to the enemy, as the time-honoured rules of war laid down. But Sir Francis cared not a whit for the quaint practices of an out-dated code of war and he despised excessive caution; his authority was supreme under the Queen's commission. That same afternoon, the fleet entered Cadiz, and Borough reluctantly followed. The Spaniards were taken completely by surprise.

Two galleys from Port St Mary, on the far side of the outer harbour, came out to investigate, but Drake crippled both of them with his culverins. He saw some sixty vessels, many of them without crews, most of them without a sail hoisted. There was utter panic. Those ships that could possibly move to the safety of the inner harbour or across to Port St Mary cut their cables; the rest fell victims to the English onslaught to be sunk, burned or taken as prizes. Resistance was negligible. Drake anchored for the night out of range of the town guns, but instead of quitting Cadiz at first light, as Borough hoped, laid his plans for devastating the inner harbour, for here he had espied the galleon belonging to the Marquis of Santa Cruz himself.

At dawn, on the flood tide, Drake from the *Merchant Royal* led a flotilla of pinnaces into the inner harbour to complete his work. He gutted the Admiral's great ship, pounded a number of other vessels and then withdrew to the relative safety of the outer harbour, where the main fleet had meanwhile been revictualling. By midday he was ready to sail, but the wind dropped completely. After so great a *coup*, in which he had captured six vessels laden with provisions and destroyed thirty-one others together with a vast amount of stores, worth little less than a million pounds, it was no time to lose his head. The Spaniards moved guns down to the sandhills, sent in two galleys to attack and launched a number of fire ships which were carried by the tide towards the English anchorage, yet the fleet proved impregnable under heavy fire, and was able to manœuvre out of the way of the fire ships by warping anchors. When he saw the fire ships, Drake remarked in high spirits, 'The Spaniards are doing our work for us by burning their own ships.' The wind for which he had been praying finally came from the land at 2 am and without delay the Admiral made sail, triumphantly leading his ships safely past the galleys and the guns at the harbour entrance. 'Having performed this valuable service', ran the account of the voyage, 'we came out of the Road of Cadiz on the Friday morning with very little loss, not worth mentioning.' A few of the enemy began to give chase but were prevented from making an effective attack since the wind again dropped, and so the English fleet anchored in safe water in full view of the town they had laid waste. Subsequently Drake challenged the Spaniards to come out and fight him and then opened negotiations for the release of prisoners he had taken with English galley slaves.

Besides the considerable damage he had inflicted on the Spanish navy, Drake had acquired first-hand information about the preparations for the Enterprise against England. He knew that Martinez de Recalde, a veteran seaman, was cruising with his squadron off Cape St Vincent, probably to be on hand to guard the returning Plate Fleet on the final stage of its journey. Drake had intercepted an order for Recalde to return to Lisbon and decided that he would now attempt to intercept his squadron, but the Spaniard succeeded in eluding him, largely because the winds were in his favour. In a calm off Cape St Vincent Drake called his officers together and announced that they would go ashore to seize Sagres Castle on the Algarve coast and, with luck, the fortified monastery nearby, which would give the fleet a foothold on the Cape – not merely a base for watering and running repairs but the command of a key point on a busy shipping route. Borough, of course, was aghast at this plan; if he thought the descent on Cadiz a gamble then to attempt Sagres was utterly feckless. Unable to convince his admiral that he was in the wrong, he next day wrote a lengthy memorandum protesting at his lack of judgment no less than his lack of respect for naval councils of war and making much of the fact that such operations were not envisaged in the sailing orders. Borough concluded: 'I pray you take this in good part, as I mean it: for I protest before God I do it to no other end but in discharge of my duty towards Her Majesty and the service.' Drake was in no mood to overlook this attempt at undermining his authority and the questioning of his professional competence and so he promptly placed the Vice-Admiral under arrest in his own ship, the *Golden Lion,* replacing him by Captain Marchant. He was convinced that Borough's example might otherwise have endangered the entire operation, for his attitude smacked of timidity.

Subsequently the crew of the *Golden Lion* mutinied to reinstate Borough in his command and the latter deserted the fleet to make for home. Drake had no alternative but to court-martial him in his absence and he was sentenced to death for mutiny and desertion. On his return to England, Drake presented a formal case against Borough to the Privy Council; a degree of timidity was indeed proven, but Borough retorted that once his former crew had overturned Captain Marchant, through lack of confidence in Drake, he had no course but to return home as a passenger. Borough was obviously not a warrior, but he had given yeoman service ashore as Clerk of the Queen's Ships over the years, and it seemed to Lord Burghley that he did not truly deserve the death sentence. The Lord Treasurer overruled Drake's recommendation, Borough went free and in the fullness of time even received his share of the prize money for the Cadiz raid.

Drake had landed at Sagres at the head of eight hundred men to storm the castle and after firing a volley of musket shots, since he had no cannon with him, he called on the captain defending the castle to surrender. When the officer refused, he started to set fire to the gates with pitch and faggots and in time a surrender was achieved. The fortified monastery of St Vincent and another neighbouring fort were subsequently taken without any show of defence and the English dismantled the guns, to remove to their ships those that could be taken away and to send the heavier artillery tumbling into the sea. 'And so they re-embarked, having secured the most important and frequented roadsted and watering place on the Atlantic coast for their own use.' While Drake was ashore at Sagres, the rest of the fleet swept from the sea any vessel that came into sight; perhaps fifty small caravels, many of them carrying staves for water casks, were plundered and fired so that the Armada became desperately short of seasoned wood for keeping fresh drinking-water.

More than satisfied with the day's work, Drake wrote that evening to his friend Walsingham at Court, imploring him to arrange for at least six more of the Queen's second-rate ships to be sent to join him forthwith. Such reinforcements would ensure that the Marquis of Santa Cruz failed to assemble his grand fleet and would enable the English to 'bring this great monarchy to those conditions which are meet'. Cadiz was not the end of the campaign, merely the end of the beginning:

OVERLEAF A Portuguese sailing ship, with the legendary 'flying fish' sighted by Magellan and others, and recorded by de Bry.

There must be a beginning of any great matter, but the continuing unto

the end until it be thoroughly finished yields the true glory. If Hannibal had followed his victories, it is thought by many he had never been taken by Scipio. God make us all thankful again and again that we have, although it be but little, made a beginning upon the coast of Spain. If we believe that this which we do is in the defence of our religion and country, no doubt but our merciful God for his Christ our Saviour's sake is able and will give us victory although our sins be red. . . . Let me be pardoned of your honour again and again for my overmuch boldness; it is the confession of my own conscience.

Lisbon was to be the next target and so Drake reorganized his fleet to make towards the mouth of the Tagus. His first impressions were that the entrance was too heavily fortified and the passage too intricate to follow without detailed local knowledge; how he wished he still had the services of Nuño da Silva whose expertise had been so invaluable on the *Golden Hind*. Even without a Borough to restrain him, Drake could readily distinguish a justifiable risk from a foolhardy show of bravado. From his anchorage in Cascaes Bay, he could see seven galleys, with their oars mounted, yet although a flat calm placed the English fleet at a serious disadvantage, none of the galleys was rowed out to do battle. Drake now sent a challenge to Santa Cruz at St Julian's Castle, which was delivered in port by a Hamburg merchantman, yet the Spaniard still would not come out and fight. Still riding unopposed at anchor 'in contempt of the said town of Cascaes', Drake demanded an exchange of prisoners of war, as he had done at Cadiz. The Marquis sent word that he had no English captives, whereupon Drake informed him that in such case he would sell his Spanish prisoners to the Moors and use the purchase money to redeem English slaves! The passage to Lisbon was too tough a nut to crack and as soon as a southerly wind came up, Drake returned to Cape St Vincent to water his ships.

He now heard that a great carrack from the East Indies was expected and so he set course for the Azores, ready to pounce. His fleet was battered by a gale and his own ship came near to foundering, while the Levant Company's ships were eager to be home. The Admiral, however, would not give up the chance of a rich prize, and sixteen days out from Cape St Vincent he came in sight of St Michael's in the Azores; as he approached more closely, he saw the outlines of a very large vessel. At dawn next day she was identified as the Portuguese carrack for which he was hunting, now sheltering in the lee of the islands. This monster was none other than the *San Felipe*, the property of Philip II himself and widely acknowledged as 'the greatest ship in all Portugal, and richly laden'. The English hailed her with cannon balls and

> having shot her through divers times, she shot at us, sometimes at one, sometimes at another. Then we began to ply her hotly, our flyboat and one of our pinnaces lying athwart her hawse, at whom she shot and threw fireworks, but did them no hurt, for that her ordnance lay so high over them. Then she seeing us ready to lay her aboard, all of our ships a-plying her so hotly and resolutely determined to make short [work] of her, six of her men being slain and divers sore hurt, they yielded unto us.

She held a massive quantity of spices and aromatic drugs, china, silks, velures, jewels and chested bullion, which was valued in England later in the year at the remarkable sum of £114,000. An English crew was put aboard the *San Felipe*, and Drake at last decided to make for Plymouth, rather than prolong his stay. This capture astounded Englishmen. 'It taught others that carracks were no such bugs, but that they might be taken' (as Richard Hakluyt choicely put it) and her precious cargo made known in London and beyond, the extensive range of the riches of the East Indies. The fact that in the last year of the century an East India Company was chartered in England, as the first step in what was to become a great empire in India, owes much to the capture by Drake of the *San Felipe* twelve years before.

On 26 June, almost three months after leaving England, Drake returned in triumph. His reputation was at its peak. 'The truth is,' wrote a foreigner, 'he has done so much damage on these coasts of Spain alone, that though the King were to obtain a most signal victory against him, he would not recover one half the loss he has suffered.' And quite apart from singeing King Philip's beard at Cadiz and Sagres, he had stolen from him his personal carrack in the Azores. Queen Elizabeth was delighted with her own share of £40,000 of the prize money no less than with his assurances that no Armada could sail for England that year. The hero himself netted £17,000, but money was not everything – indeed, plunder was for him but a secondary consideration in the Cadiz expedition. He had set out to humble Spain and crush the Armada that was being prepared, though lack of reinforcements, and of time, prevented him from carrying the wholesale destruction of Cadiz to other Spanish and Portuguese ports. In this adventure, as never before, Drake saw himself as the instrument of 'God's purpose' in rescuing England from the toils of Catholic Spain, much as Oliver Cromwell, sixty years on, would see himself as the 'sword of the

Lisbon: an engraving from J. B. Lavanha's *Viage* (1622).

Almighty'. From the anchorage at Cadiz, Drake had written a letter to John Fox, the martyrologist, which shows his Christian humility in executing what he was convinced was the divine will, and the victory belonged not to himself but to all the faithful: 'Master Fox, whereas we have had of late such happy success against the Spaniards, I do assure myself you have faithfully remembered us in your good prayers and therefore I have not forgotten briefly to make you a partaker thereof.' He called on Fox to continue his supplications and thanksgiving 'that we may have continued peace in Israel' and signed his letter 'Your loving friend and faithful son in Christ Jesus'. As a postscript he added, 'Our enemies are many, but our Protector commandeth the whole world. Let us all pray continually and our Lord Jesus will hear us in good time mercifully.' Alas, before that touching letter could be delivered, the old man who had watched Drake's extraordinary career with admiration died; and though Sir Francis was anything but a sentimental man, news that Fox had departed this life slightly soured the fruits of victory, for he had been a link with Drake's Protestant origins and with his father.

7 The Armada and After

PREVIOUS PAGES A chart showing the action of the English and Spanish fleets in the Channel and around the coast of the British Isles, taken from John Pine's *Views of the Armada* published in 1739.

BELOW The Duke of Medina Sidonia, who openly admitted that he had 'neither aptitude, ability, health, nor fortune for the expedition'.

As the year 1587 drew to a close, throughout Europe seers and astrologers were foretelling catastrophes; the new year would bring upheavals, lamentations and the ruin of empires. Francis Drake, who respected John Dee's mathematical expertise and admired his scientific approach to geographical discovery, was dubious about dismissing such portents. Dee himself was away in Germany, but as a regular reader of the Scriptures, Drake felt that these deductions from Biblical numerology and the heavens might well be valid. Some regarded the sudden death of the Marquis of Santa Cruz, whom Philip II had chosen as admiral to command the Armada, as a portent of doom. The Duke of Medina Sidonia, a thirty-eight-year-old grandee from Old Castile was appointed in his place, although largely ignorant of naval warfare and a martyr to sea-sickness. He found the extensive preparations entirely inadequate, even allowing for the destruction which Drake had wrought at Cadiz. Prophecies and all that Drake heard of developments in Spain increased his anxiety for action. He was eager to be afloat again and told a Spaniard in London during December that the next Christmas he would celebrate victoriously in Portugal. As England's preparations for victualling the fleet and overhauling ships moved forward slowly, Drake and Hawkins were alarmed that Queen Elizabeth was taking at its face value Parma's concern to negotiate for peace. 'Our profit and best course is to seek our peace by a determined and resolute war', they wrote. Parma, busily digging canals near the coast of Flanders and collecting flat-bottomed boats for the invasion of England, once the Spanish grand fleet had gained command of the Narrow Seas, was in fact no less worried about the strength of his army than Drake about the state of the English fleet.

In England there were patriotic jokes about 'proud Parma' whose military discipline was as rigid as his Catholic orthodoxy; in Spain it was Drake, above all, who was lampooned. Walsingham's spies reported the great fear in which he was held and that to keep up their spirits sailors made up songs about him. In the taverns of Spanish ports, one ballad became very popular with the crews waiting to embark. This was '*Mi hermano Bartolo*', which runs in translation:

> And Bartolo my brother
> To England forth is gone,
> Where The Drake he means to kill
> And the Lutherans every one.

> Their Queen among the first
> He will capture and bring back
> Like heretics accurst....

In December 1587 the Queen had appointed Lord Howard of Effingham, the Lord High Admiral, to command her fleet and within a few days the Council had drawn up its plan for the defence of the coasts. Drake, with seven of the Queen's ships and initially fourteen armed merchantmen, was to defend the western approaches to the Channel from Plymouth. Lord Henry Seymour was to patrol the Straits from Dover, while the Lord Admiral himself was to see to the defence of the Thames Estuary from his base at Queenborough. Drake had been allowed to select from the royal ships the one in which he would fly his flag and he chose the *Revenge*, a galleon of medium size, constructed in 1574, which he considered the ideal of what a man-of-war should be. She was a vessel of five hundred tons, compared with Howard's *Ark* and Hawkins's *Victory*, which were each of eight hundred tons burden, and she was one of the speediest ships in the fleet. Measuring ninety-two feet in length and thirty-two feet in the beam, she carried twenty-two culverins and twelve light cannon. The *Revenge* was worked by 150 mariners, assisted by twenty-four gunners and seventy-six soldiers, the last being carried chiefly to serve in boarding parties. In the 1588 campaign, the principal officers of the *Revenge* were John Grey, the master, Jonas Bodenham, the lieutenant, who was a close friend of Drake's, and Richard Derrick, the boatswain.

Ever since his return from Cadiz the previous summer, Drake had been urging that he should again be allowed to take the initiative and descend on the Spanish coast with a great force. Attack was always the best means of defence, and there was little point, he thought, in building new coastal defences in south-eastern England to prevent Parma from landing if the key to grand strategy lay in striking at Spanish shipping in its home ports. Another blow, similar to the one he had delivered at Cadiz, would both cripple the enemy and be a marvellous fillip to English morale, he wrote to the Council from Plymouth at the end of March. All the Queen's subjects would be persuaded 'that the Lord of all strength will put into Her Majesty and her people courage and boldness not to fear any invasion in her own country, but to seek God's enemies where they may be found'. He asked for fifty ships for his proposed expedition, yet on Howard's advice

FOLLOWING PAGES The well-known painting of the decisive battle of Gravelines, when the First Armada was defeated.

Elizabeth refused to let him sail, since in his absence she feared that the Channel ports would be defenceless. With the benefit of hindsight, it is clear that had Drake attacked Lisbon or another port in the spring of 1588, the Armada would not have sailed that year.

Secretary Walsingham advised him to write personally to the Queen, answering various questions she had raised, and in mid-April he sent her a characteristic letter. His crews were in wonderful spirits, he told her, eager for action, 'for I have not in my life-time known better men and possessed with gallanter minds than' those serving with him, all of them 'ready to put their hands and hearts to the finishing of this great piece of work, wherein we are persuaded that God, the giver of all victories will in mercy look upon your most excellent Majesty'. He was anxious for her to command him away to sea and so he peppered his 'humble advice' with maxims on naval strategy, which he believed to be self-evident: 'The advantage of time and place in all martial actions is half a victory; which being lost is irrecoverable.' (This could have been Blake, Nelson or Winston Churchill speaking.)

When, later in April, Drake had further intelligence about the concentration of galleons and transports at Lisbon, he wrote again to the Queen, warning her that the peace talks conducted by Parma in Flanders were a blind. England could be out of imminent danger as soon as she would let him put to sea. This letter had a marked effect, for within a few days he was summoned to Court to explain his strategy to the Council in person and, leaving Thomas Fenner in command of his squadron, he rode post haste from Plymouth to London. At the Council meeting on 10 May, he succeeding in convincing Queen Elizabeth of the soundness of his proposals, and the Lord Admiral reluctantly gave way. As a result of Drake's pressure, fresh instructions were issued, for providing more money, for provisioning the ships and for allowing Howard a far freer hand, instead of requiring him to stick like a limpet to the English coast. While still in Whitehall, Drake received a welcome letter from Fenner and his deputy, Captain Robert Crosse, assuring him that all was well at Plymouth, with his ships 'wonderfully well-manned with mariners'. 'All in generality do greatly desire your return; and in great love many of the captains and gentlemen commend them to your good favour. And so we commit you to the Lord of Lords, who preserve and keep you.' Such was the affection in which he was held.

At last Howard, flying his flag in the *Ark*, brought his fleet from

Queenborough to join Drake's in Plymouth Sound, foreshadowing a marauding expedition, but the weather was unkind; there was 'an extreme, continual storm' and the ships were so buffeted as they rode at anchor that the officers joked that they had been forced to dance 'as lustily as the gallantest dancers in the court'. Moreover, additional provisions were still awaited. By now Howard was convinced that Drake, whom he had appointed Vice-Admiral, was absolutely right in wanting to ravage the ports of Spain and Portugal and he told Secretary Walsingham 'how lovingly and kindly Sir Francis Drake beareth himself'. The Lord Admiral had feared that the unruly seadog might find it hard to play second fiddle, yet he was behaving most dutifully and deserved a warm letter of thanks from Walsingham. This makes plain the fact that it was Drake who was universally regarded as the inspiration and the effective commander of the fleet.

News arrived early in July that the Armada was at Corunna, and with the warrants to hand for purchasing additional provisions, the captains and crews were busy lading. Drake set down on paper a cogent memorandum, fully endorsed by Howard, to leave harbour as soon as the stores were aboard. 'My opinion is altogether that we shall fight with them much better cheap upon their own coast than here.' Ninety ships left the Sound on 7 July, racing towards the Bay of Biscay on a fresh north-east wind, to seek out the enemy. As they reached the north coast of Spain, the wind without warning shifted to the south and they had perforce to return home, arriving at Plymouth on 12 July, the same day on which Medina Sidonia left Corunna. It was a disappointment to be cheated of a certain victory by the fickleness of the wind, yet the expedition had been far better for morale than staying idle in harbour. This swoop towards the enemy's coast at the eleventh hour has been justly described (by Sir Julian Corbett) as the most brilliant and daring expedition ever made by a naval commander. Back in port, they took on fresh water and stores, for the southerly wind that had forced them home was assuredly bringing the enemy daily nearer England. On 19 July the skipper of an English scout-boat sent news that some Spanish vessels were off the Scillies with their sails struck, waiting for stragglers. That night Howard and Drake brought their ships out of the Sound on the ebb tide, making use of warps, to anchor them in deep water and be ready for action.

At daylight on Saturday the 20th, Howard brought fifty-four ships to leeward of the Eddystone Rocks and sailed to the south,

FOLLOWING PAGES The *Ark Royal,* originally known as the *Ark Raleigh,* but now commanded by the Lord High Admiral himself.

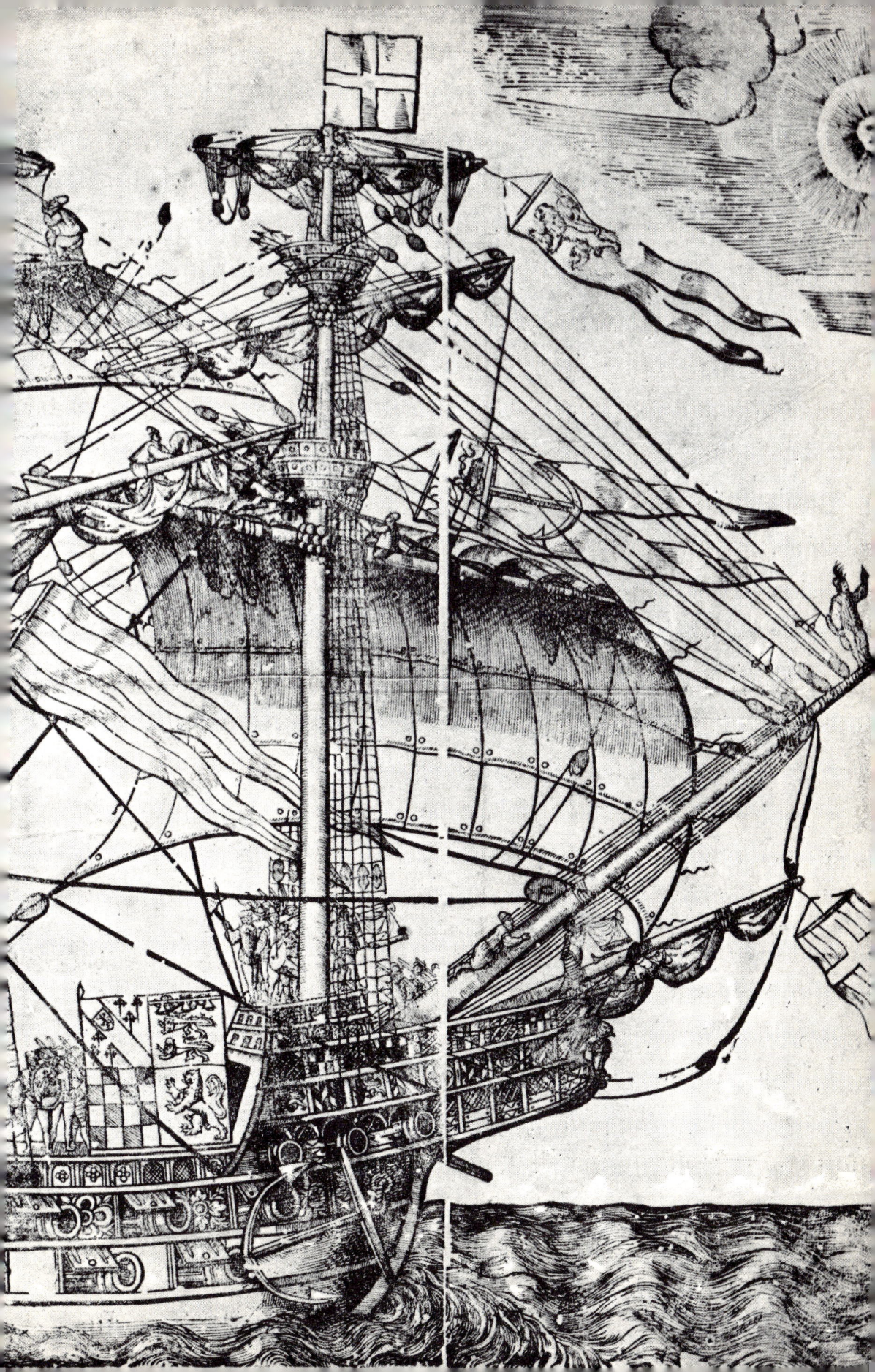

The Spanish Armada is sighted in the English Channel, off the Lizard: a scene from Pine's tapestry in the House of Lords.

to enable him, by working to windward, to double back on the enemy. Drake in the *Revenge* was positioning his eight ships to be ready to pounce on the Spanish rear. Late in the evening, he saw the enemy fleet which Medina Sidonia had formed into an enormous crescent, with the largest galleons at the points and flanks, the weakest in the middle. It was an imposing sight – this defensive formation of gigantic vessels 'with lofty towers, castle-like, in front like a crescent moon'. The galleons were elaborately painted and gilded, flying colourful banners and pennants. Majestically this great armada of 132 vessels, thirty-two of them galleons and other first-line ships, moved up the Channel. Though the English had from the first won the weather gauge, they desperately needed to get into a position in which they could use their cannon effectively.

With Frobisher and Hawkins in company, Drake prepared to attack the enemy rear, selecting for their first victim the *San Juan de Portugal*, flying the flag of the Vice-Admiral, Juan Martinez de Recalde. The English gunfire threw his ship off course so that she forced the neighbouring *Nuestra Señora del Rosario*, commanded by Don Pedro de Valdes, to foul the rigging of a third galleon. The

Rosario, crippled by the loss of her foremast and bowsprit, fell astern. That night Drake swore that he would seize the laggard as his prize. After the Armada had been defeated, Drake faced criticism for leaving his station to pursue the Spaniard; Frobisher especially was severe on him, calling it a selfish, even a traitorous, act. At any rate, Lord Admiral Howard was entirely satisfied with Drake's explanation and the Admiralty Court duly awarded Drake and his crew their prize money. (At a later stage of the action, Howard also left the line of battle to go after a prize.) To stop the rest of the fleet from following him, Drake had put out his poop lantern. On that dark night, the vessel which he thought was the *Rosario* proved to be a German merchantman. Later he found his prey and though she was much more heavily armed than the *Revenge*, the Admiral surrendered once he learned the identity of his opponent. It was not surprising that it was to Drake that the first Spanish casualty had fallen. He put some of his men aboard the *Rosario* to take her into Tor Bay, while Don Pedro and several of his officers were transferred to the *Revenge* as prisoners of war; a week later, they were put ashore at Rye and then placed in the custody of Drake's kinsman Richard Drake of Esher, with whom they were to stay for three years until ransomed. Don Pedro was

A detail of the English and Spanish fleets engaging near Plymouth, from Saxton's Atlas.

THE
𝕰𝖓𝖌𝖑𝖎𝖘𝖍 𝕸𝖊𝖗𝖈𝖚𝖗𝖎𝖊.

Publiſhed by AUTHORITIE.

For the Prevention of falſe Reportes.

Whitehall, July 23d, 1588.

EARLIE this Morninge arrived a Meſſenger at Sir *Francis Walſingham's* Office, with Letters of the 22d from the Lorde High Admirall on board the *Ark-Royal*, containinge the followinge materiall Advices.

On the 20th of this Inſtant Capt. *Fleming*, who had beene ordered to cruize in the Chops of the Channell, for Diſcoverie, brought Advice into *Plymouth*, that he had deſcried the *Spaniſh Armado* neare the *Lizard*, making for the Entrance of the Channell with a favourable Gale. Though this Intelligence was not received till near foure in the Afternoone, and the Winde at that time blew hard into the *Sound*, yet by the indefatigable Care and Diligence of the Lorde High Admiral, the *Ark-Royal*, with five of the largeſt Frigates, anchored out of the Harbour that very Eveninge. The next Morninge, the greateſt Part of her Majeſtie's Fleet gott out to them. They made in all about eighty Sail, divided into four Squadrons, commanded by his Lordſhip in Perſon, Sir *Francis Drake* Vice-Admiral, and the Rear-Admirals *Hawkins* and *Forbiſher*. But about one in the Afternoone, they came in Sighte of the Spaniſh Armado two Leagues to the Weſtward of the Eddiſtone, ſailing in the Form of a half-Moon, the Points whereof were ſeven Leagues aſunder.

ABOVE An engraving from the painting by Sir Oswald Brierly (1817–94) illustrating the capture of the *Rosario*, which Drake, in the *Revenge*, escorted to Tor Bay.

OPPOSITE The *English Mercurie* officially reports the sighting of the Armada, news which reached the English public on 23 July 1588.

to write to Philip II emphasizing the courteous treatment he had received aboard the *Revenge*. Drake had aboard a Spanish-speaking officer who was able to discover from these captives something of Medina Sidonia's plans and when the *Revenge* caught up with the main fleet later in the day, he reported these findings to Howard.

Off Start Point on the evening of 21 July, Drake wrote a letter at Howard's request, to be taken by a fast caravel to Lord Henry Seymour off Dover, giving him a brief account of the opening days' action and requiring him to be ready to join in the attack as the Armada reached the Narrow Seas. 'As far as we can perceive they are determined to sell their lives with blows'; the enemy was numerous, 'but truly I think not half of them men-of-war'. There was a brisk action off Portland Bill early on 23 July and a much greater battle, which lasted for many hours, south-east of the Isle of Wight on the following day, 'with great expense of powder and bullet' on both sides. Despite overall superiority of fire power, the English could not succeed in sinking galleons. Medina Sidonia's

Detail of the two fleets in combat off the Isle of Wight.

ABOVE Philip II of Spain, painted by Sanchez Coello: married briefly to Queen Mary, he had once hoped to gain the hand of her sister Elizabeth, for the sake of a Catholic Europe.

RIGHT The Armada portrait of Elizabeth by Gheeraerts: decked out in her customary splendour, she has witnessed England gain supremacy over the high seas.

crescent formation had proved its value. Drake almost claimed another victim, but the wind dropped at the vital moment and the *Gran Grifon* was safely towed off by a galleon to the centre of the crescent. The running fight continued up-Channel for another three days; both sides were getting short of shot, but Howard and Drake could not break the enemy's defensive formation. The Spaniards came to anchor in Calais Roads on Saturday 27 July to keep their *rendez-vous* with Parma. It was reported in Paris that 'for four days Drake continuously kept to the windward of the enemy, thanks to the better sailing of his ships, and pursued and bombarded them without ceasing. He can repeat this manœuvre as often as he pleases, for the Spanish ships are heavy and difficult to handle.' Now that the fleets had reached confined waters, given the right weather conditions, the English should be able to command the advantage.

So far, however, it was stalemate. For his part, Medina Sidonia was dismayed that the Prince of Parma had insufficient flat-bottomed craft to bring his soldiers, camped between Dunkirk and Nieuport, to the anchorage; and yet Admiral Howard could not bring his ships safely within gunshot range of the enemy. At a council of war on the *Ark*, it was decided to send in fire ships to wreak havoc in the Spanish anchorage. Most probably Drake was

BELOW The English fleet in hot pursuit of the Armada, whose ships are in the form of a crescent: another view from the Pine tapestry.

OPPOSITE The signatures of the members of the English Council of War who resolved to destroy the Armada.

2. Augusti. 1588

Forasmuch as we herunder written have determined and agreed in counsaile to followe and pursue the Spanyshe Fleete, for till we have cleared owr own coaste and browght the fyrst weste of us And her to returne backe againe aswell to repletenall our Shipps (to stand in contrari partithie) as also to guarde and defend owr own coaste at somedeth further go testatione that if we wante of victualles and munitione owr supplied we cold happ pursue them to the furtheste that they durste have gone.

Howard   George Cumberland

[signatures] Edmonde Sheffeelde

Fra: Drake   Edw Hoby

Jhō Hawkyns

Thomas Hewarde

the originator of the scheme, for he had seen fireships in use at Cadiz the previous year and the enemy from the first believed that the plan was his. At any rate, he was the first to volunteer an armed merchantman that he owned – the *Thomas*, a Plymouth ship of two hundred tons. Hawkins followed by offering one of his vessels, and soon eight ships were speedily being filled with pitch, tar, dry timber and anything that would easily burn. The guns were left aboard but were double-shotted so that they would explode from the intense heat. Before midnight on the Sunday, these fireships, lashed together, were carried by the wind and a strong tide on their mile-and-a-half voyage – pilotless phantom ships. The Spaniards had feared that the English possessed a secret weapon and here at last were the dreaded 'devil ships'. In utter confusion, the Spaniards cut their cables as the ships penetrated the cordon of fly-boats and pinnaces which protected the galleons. No galleon caught fire, but Medina Sidonia was forced out of his anchorage into the open sea, placing his fleet at the mercy of the English.

Next morning, soon after dawn, a battle began in earnest off Gravelines. Drake's squadron opened the attack by pounding the flagship, the *San Martin*, though she proved impregnable. For seven hours there was fighting at close quarters during which the English showed their superiority over their opponents in handling their ships in difficult water. Then, at 4 pm the wind changed to the north-west and there was a blinding squall. Howard called off the attack and stood his fleet out to sea while the galleons which had survived the battle seemed certain of being driven onto the perilous lee shore of the Dutch sands. That evening Sir Francis wrote in high spirits to Walsingham: 'God hath given us so good a day in forcing the enemy so far to leeward as I hope in God the Prince of Parma and the Duke of Sidonia shall not shake hands these few days; and whensoever they shall meet, I believe neither of them will greatly rejoice at this day's service.' The general verdict on the battle was that of the Venetian ambassador in Paris, who reported, 'The English have shown that they are in fact the skilled mariners which rumour reported them to be, for while they have always been on the enemy's flank, they have not lost a single ship.'

Medina Sidonia was saved from disaster early the next day by the wind's backing to west-south-west, so he could move his fleet into the deeper water of the North Sea. He decided at a council of war that if the wind changed again, he would fight his way back through the Straits of Dover and attempt to take an English harbour, to hold it for Parma; if, on the other hand, the wind stayed in the south-west, he would have no alternative but to lead the remnant of the Armada home as best he could, sailing north through the North Sea and westward around the Orkneys and Shetlands and the west of Ireland. In the event, the south-westerly wind held and so he began the long, hazardous voyage back to Spain. Howard and Drake gave chase with their squadrons, but Seymour to his dismay was ordered to patrol off Dover. Before Drake weighed anchor, he sent a further hurriedly scribbled note to Walsingham: 'There was never anything pleased me better than the seeing the enemy flying with a southerly wind to the westwards. God grant you have a good eye to the Duke of Parma, for with the grace of God, if we live, I doubt it not but ere it be long, so to handle the matter with the Duke of Sidonia as he shall wish himself at St Mary Port among his orange trees.'

Fresh victuals were sent to the English fleet, but there was a desperate shortage of ammunition. Howard and Drake still hoped to give battle as they followed in the wake of the great ships, but when the Armada had passed beyond the Firth of Forth, perhaps sixty miles from shore, they decided to give up the chase and return to the Downs. England was not yet out of danger, for Parma, Europe's greatest general, still had his army ready for embarkation if the weather proved suitable and there was a chance to elude Seymour's squadron. By the time Drake was off the north coast of Norfolk, a westerly gale had set in and though this did much damage to spars and rigging, it was clear to him that the threat from Parma was over for the present; at Tilbury Camp, however, where the main army for the defence of the realm waited with Leicester, uncertainty remained about the outcome of the naval battle and its effects on Philip of Spain's grand strategy. The day before the westerly gale buffeted the fleet, Elizabeth feared that invasion was imminent and after reviewing her army at Tilbury delivered the most famous of all her speeches.

From his anchorage in the Downs, so near the waters where as a child he had mastered the elements of seamanship, Drake wrote two more letters to Walsingham in a very shaky hand, almost overcome by sleep. He urged the Secretary that this was no time to pay off ships or disband armies for he knew his sovereign too well to imagine that she was not counting the cost of every day the emergency lasted; as he put it in a pithy phrase, 'I dare not advise Her Majesty to hazard a kingdom with saving of a little change.'

ABOVE AND FOLLOWING PAGES Some of John Pine's views of the Armada, charting the course of the two fleets as they swept eastwards through the Channel, from the Lizard right up to the Kent coast.

General of all the Army.
general of the Fleet of Biscay.
of the Fleet of Castile.
analusian Squadron.
e Guypuscoan Squadron.
der of the Levantiscas.
ander of the Hulks.
er of the Pataches & Zabra's.
four Galleasses of Naples.
four Gallies of Portugal.

After allowing himself a few hours' rest, he wrote to the Queen herself, for he was nearer the Court than Howard, who had taken the *Ark* into Dover, telling her of the fate of the Armada but reiterating how vital it was to keep her forces together. Drake thought that the galleons might have been forced by the gale towards Scandinavia and so he urged royal enquiries to be made of their ships of the King of Denmark; the Spaniards certainly needed to find a major port if they were to repair their battered vessels sufficiently to threaten England again. The Prince of Parma, Drake wrote in another despatch, was like 'a bear robbed of her whelps' and to make him banish from his mind all thoughts of invading the realm, he suggested a naval demonstration off Dunkirk, yet the Queen, as paymaster, did not want the emergency to last a day longer. It was probably only now, as a result of Drake's letter, that Elizabeth fully grasped that the battle of Gravelines was an overwhelming defeat for the Armada, and that being so, she became tetchy about the lack of plunder. She had already sent Richard Drake, an equerry who was a kinsman of the Admiral, to enquire among the fleet how much treasure had been taken in the actions and why no Spanish ships had been boarded. Now she summoned Howard to Whitehall, to order him to pay off the armed merchantmen.

Fearing that some members of the Privy Council might try to exploit any rift between himself and the Lord Admiral, Drake sent Walsingham a note which could be passed around, testifying to Howard's honourable employment of him in the action, 'wherein if I have not performed as much as was looked for, yet I persuade myself his good Lordship will confess I have been dutiful'. It was not in fact for another four days that Howard presented himself at Court and then he took both Drake and Hawkins with him.

With the fighting over, the bickering in the English fleet now began. The headstrong Frobisher had been heard attacking Drake's reputation in Lord Sheffield's house at Harwich in the presence of John Hawkins and others. In the fight, said Frobisher, Drake had behaved 'like a cowardly knave' and now was saying that 'no man hath done as good service but he'. What rankled with the Yorkshireman was Drake's prize of the *Rosario*, but others were jealous of his rank as second-in-command – a second-in-command, indeed, on whom the Lord Admiral relied so heavily that he had 'practically surrendered to him the command of the fleet'. Lord Seymour in particular nursed a grudge. After the battle of Gravelines, he had been ordered back to Dover when he felt that he should have been chasing the Spaniards in the North Sea. Howard now sent for Seymour, but the latter excused himself on the grounds that he had an independent command; he wrote in a furious temper that, if the Lord Admiral should come to the Narrow Seas with Drake as his Vice-Admiral in attendance, 'I say you let me be called home'. Certainly Sir Francis did not steal the honours of victory from his superior; yet for his part, Howard paid tribute throughout to Drake's great experience, invaluable advice and infectious courage. Most contemporaries at home and abroad regarded the defeat of the Armada as essentially Drake's victory – even Philip II, the Pope, Parma and Henry of Navarre. The Venetian envoy at Henry III's Court wrote that Drake had reported to Queen Elizabeth that *he* had left the enemy with eighty-two sail out of the original 130, and that these survivors were in great distress from battle damage and want of provisions, water and munitions.

The officers put aside their arguments to deal with another crisis. In the vessels in the Downs, typhus was rife and men were dying like flies. Under these changed circumstances, when the admirals discussed the problem of disbanding the fleet with the Queen in Council they agreed to an immediate reduction to one hundred sail, for it would have been folly, with the epidemic raging, to have kept men cramped together unnecessarily; and as soon as possible, most of the other ships would be paid off. Hurrying back to Sheerness, Drake and Hawkins divided this reduced fleet into two divisions, one stationed in the Downs, the other at Margate, to try to prevent the sickness spreading. It was seeing the plight of crews ill from typhus that led the two Plymouth professionals to found the Chatham Chest for the relief of sick and wounded seamen.

Before the end of the month, there were reports that some few of the Spanish galleons were returning into the English Channel, but Drake refused to countenance these rumours. His own 'poor opinion' was that the enemy would come back only because they were at the mercy of the winds, and would be in no shape for battle. By 10 September all but a small force, left as guardians of the Channel under Sir Henry Palmer, remained of the 197 vessels that served in the 1588 campaign. At last it was possible to survey in detail the damage done to the fleet and it was found that the *Revenge* needed a new mainmast, for the existing one had been severely weakened by enemy shot, a new capstan and pinnace. Throughout the period 1 January to 10 September, Drake had been paid as Vice-Admiral at 30s per day (compared with Howard's £3.6s.8d.) and the bill for the wages of the 2,737 men under his command came to £19,228. He took especial pains to ensure that every man, or his widow, was paid his due and that the men in the *Revenge* received their fair shares of prize money from the capture of the *Rosario*.

By 13 September the Spanish flagship, the *San Martin*, reached Santander, yet the Duke of Medina Sidonia was very weak from dysentery and could not organize relief for his men suffering from typhus and scurvy. No one praised him for achieving the remarkable feat of bringing home under the most difficult circumstances as many as sixty-seven vessels; he was in disgrace and never returned to sea. Philip II, unaware that the 'invincible' Armada had been set an impossible task, was already planning a further expedition against England.

Drake agreed to the flags and banners captured from the *Rosario* being honourably laid up in St Paul's Cathedral. He was distantly related to old Dean Nowell from whom, no doubt, the request for these trophies came, and they became one of the sights of London – especially a silken streamer depicting the Virgin and Child – until they perished with St Paul's in the Great Fire of London. The Queen and the greatest in the land had come to the Cathedral on 24 November for an impressive Thanksgiving Service for the victory, at which John Piers, Bishop of Salisbury, delivered an impassioned sermon on the theme of 'the Protestant Wind' – the same rushing, mighty wind that had once wrecked Pharaoh's chariots in the Red Sea – and the Bishop's pulpit oratory earned him promotion to the archbishopric of York. Drake, who must have been at St Paul's for the occasion, while convinced that the God of Rome, whom Philip II worshipped so piously in the chapel of the Escorial, the Lord of the Jesuits and the Inquisition, had withheld his blessings from the Spanish Crusade because the moral strength of Protestantism was self-evident, cannot have been happy about the popular theory, fast gaining acceptance, that the victory was due to the wind. In truth, at almost every stage of the campaign, the weather had favoured the Spaniards. The victorious commanders had no such recognition as Bishop Piers, and Lord Admiral Howard had to wait until 1597, after Drake's death, for his earldom. The Queen, however, made an innovation by issuing various medals to mark the victory – the first time that campaign medals were struck by an English sovereign – and most bore the inscription 'God breathed and they were scattered.'

One of the medals issued to commemorate the victory over the Armada – the first historical event for which medals were struck by an English sovereign.

At this time, Drake decided that he needed a London house, for it had been inconvenient finding lodgings every time he came to the capital for the Parliamentary session or to attend Court, and his maritime interests were increasingly involving him with negotiations with City financiers. In November 1588 he purchased a long lease of a splendid mansion in Dowgate Ward in the city, known as The Herbor (or Erbor), with a frontage on the Thames, very near the German merchants' Steelyard. The Duke of Clarence had once lived here and later his daughter, Margaret Pole, Countess of Salisbury, resided at The Herbor when she was in London, so for a time the house became known as Salisbury Place. More recently it had been occupied by a Spanish merchant, Don Querras, who had dabbled in politics until forced to leave England. Sir John Puleston, who owned the property, extensively rebuilt the house in the mid-1580s so that it was one of the newest and most splendid residences in the city. Drake liked being near the river, enjoyed the gardens and had ample space for entertaining, and as a result of acquiring the house, his wife came from Buckland to

Sir John Norris, who took part in the unsuccessful Portugal expedition. Unlike Drake, however, he quickly regained the Queen's confidence.

London much more often. The Herbor had been demolished before the end of the seventeenth century and today the site is occupied by Cannon Street Station.

Almost as soon as the fleet which fought the Armada had been paid off, the Queen was under pressure from Drake and Hawkins to carry the war into enemy territory. There was the splendid chance of utterly destroying the galleons which had crept home to Biscayan ports for refitting, and a widespread swoop on these and other harbours would not merely prevent Philip II from sending a further Armada against England but bring him to his knees to sue for peace. Elizabeth saw the force of her captains' argument but she was in too low financial water to bear the total cost of such an expedition. She much preferred the rival plan of sending out a small squadron to intercept one of the Spanish treasure-ships in the Azores for, if successful, this could at a stroke provide a rich return for her investment. Drake weaned her from this plan and instead persuaded her that, with his new contacts in the city, she could expect to delegate to a joint stock company the main financing of a voyage to the Peninsula.

Her Majesty would, of course, be a major shareholder and would retain the prerogative of issuing the commanders with their instructions, but the bulk of the money would be subscribed by others. As a result of the Queen's enthusiasm, the plans for the Portugal Expedition hardened and as early as 19 October, Drake and Sir John Norris were named as joint commanders. While the details were being worked out, Drake served on a committee to advise on a naval construction programme. This committee recommended the laying down of four new capital ships, including two sister-ships of the *Revenge*.

Drake had never been so busy ashore – too busy to worry about Lord Howard of Effingham's jealousy at being supplanted from the command of the fleet. Sir Francis aimed at a complete annihilation of Spanish maritime power, as the climax of a life-time's personal endeavour in which the battle of Gravelines had been merely, as it were, an episode. His own company subscribed £5,000, while the Queen advanced £20,000 and lent six of her 'second sort of ships'. In this combined operation by sea and land, England's Dutch allies were to provide transports for the soldiers. London merchants whom Drake had persuaded to put up money looked for considerable dividends from the plunder to be captured. Never had it been so easy to recruit soldiers and sailors so that in the end perhaps twice as many sailed in the fleet as had been originally intended, upsetting the victualling arrangements. Sir John Norris, commander of the land forces, was not just a favoured son of a warm friend of the Queen, Lady Norris of Rycote, but a professional soldier of the first rank whom Drake had known in Ireland in years gone by. More recently he had served as colonel of the English volunteers who had come to the aid of the Dutch to fight alongside William the Silent, and of late he had won golden opinions for his leadership in the Netherlands campaign against Parma. 'Black John Norris', a professional warrior to the hilt, unruly and reckless, was in many ways a military counterpart to Drake. He, like the Admiral, was an innovator, and in the Portugal Expedition, for the first time, an English army was organized on the regimental system.

The Queen had tied the commanders to detailed instructions. First of all, the expedition was to destroy Spanish shipping in Santander, San Sebastian and the other Biscayan ports and then the fleet was to deal with the shipping in the River Tagus. If conditions in Portugal were favourable, they were to reinstate Don Antonio, the ex-King, who had been in exile in England for the past eight years, but if there was no hope of his restoration, the fleet was to proceed to the Azores and occupy the islands as a base for operations against the Spanish Plate Fleet. Men-of-war, armed merchantmen and transports numbered as many as 150 vessels in which perhaps over 23,000 men embarked. Drake again flew his flag in the *Revenge*.

This grand fleet forming England's own Armada was to have sailed on 1 February, but difficulties over provisioning and in waiting for the Dutch transports delayed matters and then contrary winds again postponed departure from Plymouth until 18 April. Against instructions, which had required him first to sack the ports on the Bay of Biscay, Drake began by attacking Corunna. Here he burned several ships and plundered the lower town, but the army failed to capture the more strongly fortified upper town. A store of wine on which the men laid their hands proved, literally, fatal. Having re-embarked his men, Norris was taken down the coast to land at Peniche, forty miles north-west of Lisbon. It would have been more effective to have forced the entrance to the Tagus, but conditions were unfavourable. Yet all element of surprise had gone in Norris's march towards the Portuguese capital and it was a gruelling experience for the soldiers in intense heat. There was not the slightest show of support for Don Antonio's cause and the Cardinal Archduke, iron-handed governor of

Lisbon, harried the inhabitants into defending the city. Drake had meanwhile bombarded Cascaes on the Tagus and here Norris embarked such of his troops as had survived sickness on the march. The only redeeming feature of the fighting was Drake's seizure of sixty trading vessels from Hamburg, laden with corn and naval stores.

All that Elizabeth heard of the expedition dismayed her. The Queen's anger was all the greater since her favourite, Robert Devereux, Earl of Essex, in flagrant disobedience had stolen away from Court to join the *Swiftsure* at Falmouth. Messengers failed to secure his return and Elizabeth's peremptory command for him to go ashore and ride back to London to be by her side took two months to deliver. He achieved his ambition to be in the thick of the fight, but when the generals in Portugal at last received the royal command for him to be shipped home, they obeyed forthwith for the Queen had made plain 'if you do not, ye shall look to answer for some of your smart, for these be no childish actions'. Essex was home before the rest of the fleet and, such was his hold over Elizabeth, was soon forgiven for his rashness; the next English expedition to the Peninsula, in 1596, would be under his command. Drake burned Vigo on the way home and despite rampant sickness in the fleet was prepared to undertake further ravaging, but gales scattered the fleet and even the *Revenge* sprung a serious leak. It may be that as few as six thousand of the 23,000 men returned alive from the Portugal expedition, and the plunder and prizes were valued at a mere £30,000. The descent on Lisbon was an inglorious chapter in naval history compared with the brilliance of Cadiz in 1587 or the dogged fight of Gravelines and, though Drake had done his best to follow his rigid instructions, once home he was accused of blunders and lack of judgment. Howard who had relied on him so heavily in the Armada campaign had been saved by not having the command at Lisbon and he did nothing to hide his private satisfaction that England's hero had fallen from his pedestal. It took Drake almost five years to live down the failure of the expedition.

FOLLOWING PAGES The contemporary Armada Chart showing the homeward course of the First Armada.

8 The Sun's Fellow Traveller

ELIZABETH WAS BITTERLY DISAPPOINTED at the outcome of the Portugal expedition. Far from emulating the descent on Cadiz of 1587, England's Armada had fallen rather flat, and she rated the joint-commanders for going to places 'more from profit than for service'. When she heard of the raid on Corunna, she reminded Drake and Norris of their solemn promises that their 'principal action should be to take and distress the King of Spain's navy and ships in ports where they lay; which if ye did not, ye affirmed that ye were counted to be reputed traitors'. The opportunity of preventing a resurgence of Spanish sea-power had been lost, the plunder from prizes netting a paltry £30,000 and English casualties sustained being extremely heavy. Raleigh characteristically championed the commanders and said that if only the Queen had given them a free hand, Philip of Spain would have been reduced to 'a King of figs and oranges'; sometimes her instructions had shown the worst limitations of an armchair strategist, but for the mishaps of the 1589 expedition one must fairly blame the men of action. On their return, Elizabeth put on a brave face and publicly thanked Drake and Norris for their service: 'We cannot but acknowledge ourselves infinitely bound unto Almighty God in that it hath pleased him in his great goodness and mercy to bless your attempt' and she acknowledged that they had accomplished 'as much as true valour and good conduct could achieve'. But it was soon common knowledge that Drake was in disgrace. The Queen had always been fond of the Norris family and so Sir John soon had fresh employment; Essex, too, she readily forgave for daring to join the expedition once he was back at her side. Drake became the scapegoat for the mismanaged campaign and went home to Buckland Abbey to lick his wounds.

Even if he were not to be given a fresh command at sea, there was still work to absorb his energies. Drake was busy superintending the new works for the fortification of Plymouth and preparing fireships in case another Armada sailed from Spain. At this time, too, he achieved his long-cherished project of bringing Plymouth a fresh water supply. Water was drawn from the River Meavy into a channel (or leat) that flowed for twenty-seven miles along the natural contours of the land right into the city. When the sluice was opened, Sir Francis rode alongside the leat as the water flowed, with trumpets sounding. The last day of April soon became celebrated as the Leat Feast, at which the city fathers drank from a goblet of water and then from a goblet of wine, to the toast 'May the descendants of him who gave us water never want

PREVIOUS PAGES Drake's wooden chest, showing the *Golden Hind* inlaid on the lower side of the lid, now at Berkeley Castle in Gloucestershire.

An engraving of Elizabeth I towards the end of her reign.

for wine.' Drake also took over from the Hawkins family the town mills and built six additional mills for grinding corn.

The only voyage he made in 1590 was to reconnoitre the coast of Brittany to learn the strength of the Spanish army near Blavet which was forcing Henry of Navarre to fight on two fronts. When the Queen finally agreed to send an expedition to intercept the Spanish treasure fleet in 1590, it was Hawkins and Frobisher who were given the command, while Drake was passed over and saw Frobisher flying his flag in the *Revenge*. In view of their lack of success, caused partly by friction between the two commanders and partly by Frobisher's timidity, Drake may well have been thankful that he was not involved, but it was galling to see an opportunity lost.

Sir Martin Frobisher: he was mortally wounded when he and Norris led an expedition to relieve Crozon in Brittany, then in the hands of the Spanish, in 1594.

Like Hawkins, Drake underestimated the revival of Spanish sea-power which the reverses of 1586–8 had stimulated. Philip II had launched a massive ship-building programme, so that his fleet was stronger than ever. Improved artillery and better training gave his seamen fresh confidence after the failure of the Armada campaign. Some even said that they could be more daring and take greater chances against the English since they knew that Drake was kept ashore. At the same time, Pedro Menendez Marques, son of the Admiral, designed at Havana a new, fast vessel, the *gallizabra*, which could carry bullion from the Caribbean to Spain without need of a string of escorts. The days of the Plate Fleet convoys were passing and with them the chances of easy prey. Just as Drake was improving the fortifications at Plymouth Sound, so every Spanish governor in the Americas was making sustained efforts to strengthen the coastal defences.

Drake felt even less happy in 1591 when Lord Thomas Howard and Sir Richard Grenville left Plymouth for the Azores. Compared with his experience of command, these were untried men and it seemed as if he were permanently put out to grass. In turn, his chief supporters at Court, Leicester, Walsingham and finally Hatton, had died and there was no one to stand up to Lord Admiral Howard of Effingham who was now undisputed in giving advice in council, where he sat much as a minister of defence, while his wife remained the woman closest to the Queen. It was only natural that their nephew, Lord Thomas Howard, should be preferred to the Devonshire freebooter whom men said was getting too old for campaigning. Yet personal disappointment and envy had not diminished Drake's loyalty. He actively furthered the preparations for Hawkins and Grenville to follow where he had led, since as warriors fighting the good fight they needed every encouragement, and his own evangelism was as strong as ever. He applauded as a superb action Grenville's heroism at Flores, when the news reached him, whereas some denigrated his gallantry and thought it a wanton waste of life. It was eerie for Drake, as Grenville's successor at Buckland, to learn the fate of his *Revenge* of the 1588 campaign. He still fervently hoped that England would return to the offensive at sea, in both Europe and America, and as the months went by prayed that he might have another chance of influencing her to shape a glorious policy which would bring Philip of Spain to his knees.

Raleigh was allowed to launch an expedition to the West Indies to attack the Plate Fleet off Panama on lines that were intended to follow closely Drake's own classic marauding. When Raleigh was sixty leagues from port, the Queen, who had contributed two of her ships, replaced him by Frobisher. Raleigh now heard news that the treasure ships would not sail that year and in defiance of his orders sent Frobisher towards the Spanish coast while Sir John Burrough, general of land forces in the expedition, was to tarry in the Azores; the favourite reluctantly made for home to find himself sent to the Tower for his secret marriage with Bess Throckmorton, a maid of honour. Burrough succeeded in taking the richest prize of the century – the *Madre de Dios*, a great Portuguese carrack of sixteen hundred tons, homeward bound from the East Indies, her seven decks laden with a cargo of jewels, spices, ivory and silks worth £150,000 in the currency of the day, before embezzlement began. When the prize was brought into Dartmouth in September 1592, it was obvious that her riches had already been heavily pilfered by the privateers. The Queen, anxious to secure the lion's share of the plunder, appointed commissioners to seize the rest before it was too late and to cross-examine the crews.

Drake was the first commissioner on the scene but could make no headway with the seamen at Dartmouth who were near mutiny in their concern to cling to their perquisites. Perhaps £100,000 worth of precious stones and cloves had already been removed. Of the three commissioners, he was the most unpopular with the seamen who felt that they were only following in his privateering footsteps. He certainly saw the force of their argument and persuaded his fellows, Robert Cecil and Richard Hawkins, to report to Her Majesty their inability to carry out her instructions for it was 'an offence to God to put the seamen on their oath'. Drake was naturally accused of looking too kindly on the looters, but he saw that rough justice was done and the Queen received some £60,000 as the return on her own investment of £3,000.

The capture of the *Madre de Dios*, like Reneger's seizure half a century earlier, produced a new wave of privateering. Many of the men now taking to the seas were amateurs – courtiers hoping to cash in on the successes of George Clifford, Earl of Cumberland, fishermen, yeomen farmers in coastal shires dreaming of easy wealth and the dregs of the dockyards. Francis Drake steered clear of these run-of-the-mill ventures. He had had his fill of risking all for a prize in the grey areas between privateering and piracy and was now too wealthy to worry; but as a professional seaman, it irked him to have to stay ashore. He was, as always, anxious to come to grips with wider questions of sea power and national defence. At last, in November 1592, he was summoned to Court 'about some sea service' and though both Lord Thomas Howard and Martin Frobisher were present, 'Drake carrieth it away from them all.' It was like old times.

On New Year's Day, he presented Queen Elizabeth with a finely-bound account of his raid on Nombre de Dios in 1572. In his leisure ashore, he had worked hard at this narrative, which was to form the basis of the publication brought out by his nephew in 1626 as *Sir Francis Drake Revived*. Though he found literary composition 'troublesome' – and this was 'the first fruits' of his pen – his was a businesslike account of his voyage with few frills and was clearly based on his log. Some preliminary work had been done by Philip Nichols, a preacher, who perhaps 'ghosted' the opening sentences and provided the fashionable euphuism about the emmet's choler and the eagle laying her eggs in Jupiter's lap, which would strike an appreciative chord with the Queen. His presentation volume was not, however, written in the vein of an old man reliving his days of glorious action, but was a tract for the times. Drake desperately hoped to sail again under royal patronage. In the prefatory letter to Her Majesty in which he playfully charted his career, like a navigator pricking his course, he hinted broadly how much he would prefer rendering fresh service to harping on the old:

I have thought it necessary myself, as in a card [chart] to prick the principal points of the counsels taken, attempts made and success had, during the whole course of my employment in those services against the Spaniard; not as setting sail for maintaining my reputation in men's judgement, but only as sitting at helm, if occasion shall be, for conducting the like actions hereafter.

The rumour was of a new expedition to Panama and Nombre de Dios, that 'treasure house of the world', and Drake planned to land an army there which would march across the Isthmus to capture Panama. John Hawkins was brought into the discussions at Court, but there were to be many changes of plan before the fleet left, for Elizabeth still feared that another Armada might be sent against England and remained anxious about Spanish designs on Brest. If Brest fell, English command of the Channel would be most seriously threatened. (Frobisher was to be killed in operations off the Brittany coast in 1594.)

With no children of his own, Sir Francis had made much of his godson, the child of his friend — and very probably a distant cousin — Richard Drake of Esher in Surrey. The boy had been named Francis and it had been tacitly assumed that the Admiral would make him his heir. It was Richard Drake who was assigned the custody of Don Pedro and his colleagues taken prisoner from the *Rosario*, and during their stay at Esher, Sir Francis and his wife paid them frequent visits and so saw much of young Francis, then in his early teens. When, however, Thomas Drake, the Admiral's youngest brother, married and in the month following the defeat of the Armada, became a father, relations between Esher and Buckland Abbey became somewhat cooler. Eventually, Richard Drake decided that it would be sensible to send his son to stay in Devon with the great man in 1593. At the end of twelve weeks, still nothing had been said, so the boy's tutor, a Mr Pomfret, delicately broached the subject and Sir Francis asked him to make it quite plain to Richard that it would not be possible for him to settle any of his estates upon his son, because of a compact with his father-in-law, Sir George Sydenham, who would 'take it amiss' if he carved off a portion of his wife's dower. But Sir Francis did present the boy with a jewel and a purse of money when he left and hoped that father and son would understand the situation. Though Richard Drake was to be appointed an overseer of Sir Francis's will, he received no legacy. Nephew Francis, however, was destined to become the head of the family; his father was to die in 1606 when he was seventeen and before the end of James I's reign he had been created a baronet.

Drake was returned as a member of Parliament for Plymouth in February 1593 and was in his seat to hear Robert Cecil, with whom he was now on intimate terms, present the Subsidy Bill for extensive taxation to meet the cost of the war. In the long debate, Sir George Carey told members that Her Majesty was resolved to send Drake with a great navy against the Spaniards, while Sir Francis himself spoke vehemently against 'the King of Spain's strength and cruelty'. He served on the committee for the bill for providing relief for sick and wounded soldiers and sailors which continued the work of the Chatham Chest.

At last, in January 1595, the Queen commissioned Drake and Hawkins jointly to undertake a large-scale raid on the Caribbean to 'offend our capital enemy, the King of Spain'. It was because she could not now trust Drake implicitly that she harnessed him with Hawkins. As Thomas Maynarde, who sailed with them, put it, since Drake had habitually acted 'as a child of fortune, it may be his self-willed and peremptory command was doubted'. John Hawkins, long past his prime and latterly broken by misfortune, now found himself serving with his cousin for the first time since the fight at San Juan de Ulua in 1568. It was not on the face of it a happy partnership; yet the news that Drake was to sail again had an electric effect on Plymouth and beyond. Men came to volunteer their service under him, as seamen or soldiers, in such numbers that the pressed men could all be dismissed.

Drake still hankered after his scheme for sacking Panama and holding it as an English stronghold, but Elizabeth could not make up her mind. She feared that while they were in the New World, England would be defenceless. Let them first sail to the Spanish coast to destroy any galleons they met with and to keep a sharp look-out for the Plate Fleet, before they left for the Indies. Moreover, they must solemnly undertake to be back in Plymouth by May 1596. The commanders had been assembling their forces in the Sound on the understanding that they were to engage in amphibious operations in the West Indies, for which they had been recruiting soldiers and hiring transports; yet now their

Richard Drake, whose son Francis would have inherited the great seaman's wealth but for the marriage of Thomas Drake, Sir Francis's brother.

OVERLEAF PAGES London, England's capital and principal port where many of the plans for naval exploration and warfare were hatched, although the fleets generally left from Plymouth.

Queen was altering the entire plan of campaign, with talk of naval battles off the Peninsula and hunting for the Plate Fleet. Since Elizabeth was providing six of her finest warships, including the *Garland* and the *Defiance*, and was investing £30,000 in the operations, it was imperative to retain her goodwill. While they assured her of their readiness to spend their lives in her service, they told her that she was expecting the impossible, for their fleet was not fitted to execute the revised plan. If at this late stage she wanted to launch an expedition to seek naval actions against a mighty fleet and go hunting for prizes, then she must bear the

whole cost of it herself and her commanders would do their utmost to reorganize their forces to suit such operations.

The commanders shrewdly sought the support of young Essex, the Queen's favourite, in pleading their case and 'if Her Majesty do alter our first agreement, you stand strongly for us'. Thanks to the Earl's intervention, Elizabeth ruled that they need not visit the coast of Spain, but she would not retract over the time-table – they must be back in port by May 1596; and, as if the delays in departure were solely due to them, she chided them for being laggard. When they reiterated that the date of their return depended on God's blessing, she reprimanded them for calling on the Almighty to cover up 'an uncertain and frivolous answer'. Intelligence reaching Spain that Drake was preparing to leave with a mighty fleet provoked heavy desertions, while there was a general exodus from Lisbon where the inhabitants feared another raid. 'El Draque' was still the devil incarnate for simple folk in the Peninsula; 'his name is more feared here than ever Talbot's was in France', reported a spy in the weeks when the ships were victualling at Plymouth.

The expedition would have sailed at the end of July but for a sudden panic in the West. Four Spanish galleons from Brittany came into Mount's Bay in Cornwall to land six hundred men, who proceeded unopposed to lay waste the villages of Mousehole and Newlyn and the town of Penzance, firing houses and churches. Some feared a large-scale invasion, but it was soon obvious that this was no more than a side-show and when the Spaniards learned that Drake's fleet had not yet sailed, they rapidly returned to their base in Brittany. Even now the voyage was in danger of being cancelled, but Drake and Hawkins suddenly had news that a

lone galleon of the Mexican Plate Fleet, laden with bullion worth 2,500,000 ducats, had been forced by gales to shelter in Puerto Rico and it would take longer for her to be repaired than for the English to reach her. They speedily sent word to the Queen that the crippled treasure-ship 'lieth in our way and will in no way impede us' and this letter with its tenuous promise of booty swung Elizabeth round to give permission to sail. Drake and Hawkins left Plymouth Sound on 29 August with a crowd cheering from the Hoe and guns signalling 'Godspeed'. Neither would see England again.

This was a far stronger fleet than Drake had taken to the West Indies in 1585, for besides the Queen's six warships there were twenty-one heavily armed merchantmen, manned by fifteen hundred seamen, and a force of a thousand soldiers under Sir Thomas Baskerville, an able colonel, who had won honours in the Brest campaign. Sir Thomas Gorges, who had ridden to Plymouth as the Queen's messenger, reported at Court that the two Admirals 'do agree very well', but such was wishful thinking. They made an ill-assorted pair and, effectively, Hawkins in the *Garland* and Drake in the *Defiance*, commanded separate fleets. The younger man was impatient and confident of his superiority, the other cautious and ill at ease. Hawkins, wrote Maynarde, was 'old and wary, entering into matters with so leaden a foot that the other's meat would be eaten before his spit could come to the fire'. Drake required all vessels under his command to hold divine service twice daily, to forbid gambling and to keep to their proper stations in company. At a council of officers off Cape St Vincent, the two commanders would have come to blows, had it not been for Baskerville's restraining hand. Hawkins wanted to make

Plymouth: a sketch showing the compass which Drake erected on the Hoe while he was Mayor.

straight for Puerto Rico, but Drake was determined to attack Las Palmas in the Canaries, to boost morale and obtain extra provisions because, as so often, he had overmanned his fleet. After much argument, Drake had his own way.

They reached Las Palmas on 26 September, coming to anchor at the west of the harbour, not far from the fort above the town, but too heavy a surf was running to put the soldiers ashore that day and thus the element of surprise was lost. For four days, Baskerville tried to take the fort but found it impregnable; here, as also in the West Indies, as Drake would discover, the Spanish defence system had been vigorously strengthened. He now sailed round to the lee side of the island where his ships took on water undisturbed, but a party which penetrated too far inland was captured and betrayed the destination of the fleet. This was a miserable beginning to the enterprise, and the ill luck held. By the end of October all but two of the ships were at Guadalupe to water, prepare their launches and pinnaces for landing and mount the extra guns. The day after their arrival, however, five Spanish *gallizabras* came into sight. They had been sent out from Spain to bring home the treasure from the damaged vessel that had taken refuge at Puerto Rico. This was an unwelcome sight, for the Spaniards captured one of the laggard armed merchantmen from Drake's flotilla and chased the other one into the anchorage. The enemy could assess the strength of the English expedition lying in harbour and left at once for Puerto Rico to give timely warning of the coming attack. Drake, in character, was anxious to give chase, but Hawkins obstinately resisted and Drake could see that his cousin was seriously ill.

After four days, they left for the Virgin Islands where their ships could lie hidden while they prepared for action. Baskerville exercised the troops ashore while Drake scouted for fresh passages between the islets that could take the fleet to Puerto Rico. Thanks to his careful survey, on the morning of 12 November, his ships were able to arrive unheralded, weaving their way through unconventional channels to anchor in a sandy bay to the east of the town. Yet the Spanish had reinforced the defences with many additional cannon, and extra troops had been sent to beat off any attack on the citadel where the treasure lay. As the English fleet anchored, with the guns from the fort blazing, John Hawkins died, having in his last hours begged a captain to assure the Queen of his continued devotion to her service and of his despair at the ill success attending his last venture. To atone for his share in persuading her to send the expedition, he would ask her to accept a legacy of £2,000.

There was no time for lamentation. Already a shot from the shore batteries had crashed through the cabin of the *Defiance* where the officers were at supper and Drake had his seat shot from under him, while two comrades, Sir Nicholas Clifford and Brute Brown were mortally wounded. 'Ah, dear Brute', Drake exclaimed as his friend sank to the deck, 'I could grieve for thee, but now is no time for me to let down my spirits!' In the face of disaster, he remained calm, moving all the fleet out of range of the Spaniards' guns, and from a pinnace reconnoitred the coast for a likely landing-place. That night, Baskerville led in his men but the defence was far too strong for them and after an hour of heavy casualties they were forced to withdraw. Drake still did not give up the attempt and moving his ships outside the harbour next day, planned a further attack, keeping up the spirits of his men in a marvellous way. The Spanish admiral, as a desperate move, had sunk two frigates to block the entrance and at a council of war Drake reviewed the situation. Some of the younger officers were convinced that Puerto Rico was easily worth a further attempt in view of the treasure it contained, but Drake grandly told them 'I will bring you to twenty places more wealthy and easier to be gotten.' No man disputed this claim and so they left by night to find an isolated spot for watering and repairing damage. With Hawkins gone, he was at last his own master. He was determined once more to sack Panama and *en route* he would revisit the ports of the Main which he knew better than any Englishman.

On 18 December he sacked Rio de la Hacha, the scene of the earliest reverse of his career; this settled a personal score and also helped improve the morale of his men. It made him feel twenty years younger. Though the inhabitants had hidden all their valuables, the English discovered most of them and while the soldiers under Baskerville roamed the neighbouring villages, Drake raided the headquarters of the pearl fisheries and opened negotiations with the citizens of Rio de la Hacha for a ransom. Since the governor would not treat with him, Drake razed the town to the ground, sparing only two buildings, the church and the house of a lady who had implored mercy. Two days later, he took Santa Maria, though nothing of value was found, for it had been warned of the English approach, and then Sir Francis decided that Cartagena was too strongly held to be taken.

Two days after Christmas, Nombre de Dios fell to Drake for the second time and Baskerville began leading his men on the perilous march in pouring rain towards Panama. After three days of marching, however, he was forced by a well-armed Spanish force to retreat and returned with less than half his men to the ships. Drake was scarcely able to hide his acute depression. 'Since our return from Panama', noted one of his company, 'he never carried mirth nor joy in his face.' Yet he pulled himself together and at a council of war unrolled a chart to point in turn to Truxillo in Honduras and the forts on the Nicaraguan coast. Which should be their objective? 'Both! One after the other', cried Baskerville, as confident as ever in his Admiral, and Drake nodded assent; here indeed was a man after his own heart. They set sail, but contrary winds forced them to come to anchor by the isle of Escudo de Veragna in the Mosquito Gulf, to the west of Porto Bello, and here they tarried, waiting on the wind. It was a pestilential place and men went down like flies from dysentery and fever. This was certainly not the 'delicious and pleasant arbor' of the Indies, as he remembered it, but he would not admit defeat, that his judgment had been at fault or that it would be impossible even now to retrieve his reputation. 'God hath many things in store for us', he said, 'and I know many means to do Her Majesty good service and to make us rich, for we must have gold before we see England.' Then Drake himself became stricken with dysentery and had to take to his cabin. The wind still stayed in the west and after a further three days, he gave from his bed the order to weigh anchor and 'to take the wind as God had sent it'.

He became delirious on the night of 27 January and in his illness muttered a string of seaman's obscenities. With a tremendous effort, he rose from his bed to dress himself and called for his servant Whitelocke to help him into his armour, for he meant to die like a soldier. That accomplished, he was to put to bed again and in the early hours of 28 January 1596 Drake died, at peace with the world. A few hours later, the fleet came to anchor again at Nombre de Dios. Baskerville had his body laid in a leaden coffin, which was carried out from shore for sinking in the Bay, with trumpets sounding, the Admiral's three drums beating their lament and 'all the cannons in the fleet were discharged according to the custom of all sea funeral obsequies'. The Bay was a fitting burial-ground since it was 'almost in the same place where he began to grow famous to the world by his fortunate successes'. As another mark of singular honour, two ships of his own fleet and his most recent prizes were sunk near to the coffin. A verse written by a Winchester schoolboy in the excitement of the return of the *Golden Hind* would serve as an epitaph:

> The Stars above will make thee known
> If men here silent were
> The Sun himself cannot forget
> His fellow-traveller

Sir Thomas Baskerville did not delay his departure from the Spanish Main. Though he had to fight off the Spanish fleet sent to intercept him south of Cuba, he was still back in Plymouth towards the end of April, thus honouring the promise which Drake had made to the Queen. Although there was rejoicing in the Americas and in Old Spain, with Seville illuminated, when news of Drake's death arrived, before the remnant of the expedition was back in England, Howard of Effingham, the Lord Admiral, and Essex, the favourite, had left with a mighty fleet to attack Cadiz in the tradition which Drake had established. The great hopes for this new expedition in some measure compensated for the disasters of Drake's final voyage, which had lost England her two greatest seamen, and the shareholders a large sum of money.

The previous August, before leaving port, Drake had drawn up a fresh will, since he was 'now called into action by Her Majesty, wherein I am to hazard my life as well in the defence of Christ's Gospel as for the good of my Prince and Country'. The day before he died, he signed the document, adding a codicil appointing his brother Thomas sole executor, in place of the original three, with authority to sell Yarcombe Manor to Francis Drake of Esher for £2,000 in order to raise money to settle his debts, and these last-minute arrangements were to cause considerable trouble and provoke a crop of lawsuits. His widow received a life interest in Buckland and the mills in Plymouth, and his brother Thomas the fine house in Plymouth in which he was living. Lady Drake was indeed well provided for and did not long remain a widow, taking as her second husband Sir William Courtenay of Powderham, a widower. Ten years after Drake's death, his nephew and godson Francis, the son of Thomas, succeeded to Buckland and a vast inheritance. The Admiral's servant Jonas Bodenham and his secretary William Spencer received £100 apiece and all his other servants sums according to their rank and length of service. He also remembered the poor of Plymouth; but for the remarkable development of his character and the happy turn of the wheel of fortune, he might himself have ended his days as a Plymouth pauper.

Drake's Home Town

The little town of Plymouth had associations for Drake from the start to the finish of his life. His family had fled there when he was a child, to seek refuge with their Protestant relatives, only to find it in the hands of Catholic insurgents; he had set off for all his major expeditions from it; and finally he became its Mayor in 1581. The town now boasts many reminders of its world-famed hero.

LEFT The statue of Drake, compasses in hand, at Plymouth.

ABOVE Drake's drum, bearing his coat of arms, now at Buckland Abbey. Legend has it that in times of danger it beats out a warning – on his deathbed Drake promised to return at its signal.

BELOW A model of the *Golden Hind* at Buckland Abbey.

'World-admired Drake', the poets lauded him; his name had become legendary even in his own lifetime, with memories of Panama, of the voyage of the *Golden Hind* and the capture of the *Cacafuego*, of the vivid scene at Deptford and the popular conviction that the Armada's defeat was Drake's personal victory. After the adventurer had gone, the legends multiplied, though it was not until the middle of the next century that Thomas Fuller set down for the first time the story of the game of bowls on Plymouth Hoe. Drake had been incredibly popular. Ordinary folk marvelled at his achievement since for fifteen years he had embodied, even more than the Queen he served, England's determination to overcome the Colossus of Spain. There was envy and admiration at this self-made millionaire in a materialistic age. William Camden, the annalist, who began his 'obituary notice' of Drake by pouring scorn on his pillaging, went on to record that 'the vulgar sort of people honoured him with admiration and praises who thought it no less honourable to have enlarged the bounds of the English glory than those of their Empire'. He was *par excellence* a national hero, whose earthier qualities were appreciated much more readily than the aristocratic chivalry of that other hero Sir Philip Sidney.

His seamanship was superb and in days when high-ranking naval commanders, such as Howard of Effingham or Medina Sidonia, could be ignorant of fundamental aspects of ship handling, and many high-born privateers left crucial decisions to their sailing masters, Drake was a professional through and through, who had acquired his extensive knowledge in the stern school of practical experience. This professionalism included the mastery of a fast-changing body of knowledge about navigation and the ability to use scientific instruments, without which a voyage of circumnavigation would have been a fool's errand. He was passionately concerned to keep nautical information up-to-date and was patient over the details of correcting charts and sketching the views from seaward of a strange coastline. His powers of leadership and command were second to none and if he could not inspire men in the way in which Sidney, the Shepherd Knight, had attracted devoted followers, he still possessed a curiously magnetic personality which strengthened the doubting and the faint-hearted, for he was fearless and prepared to endure the rigours of the seas until the Devonshire coast hove into sight once more. He would brook no questioning of his command and, dark though the Doughty episode appears, the trial and execution of a

Anthony Ashley's *The Mariners Mirrour*, a textbook on navigation, dedicated to Sir Christopher Hatton and giving prominence to the achievements of Howard and Drake.

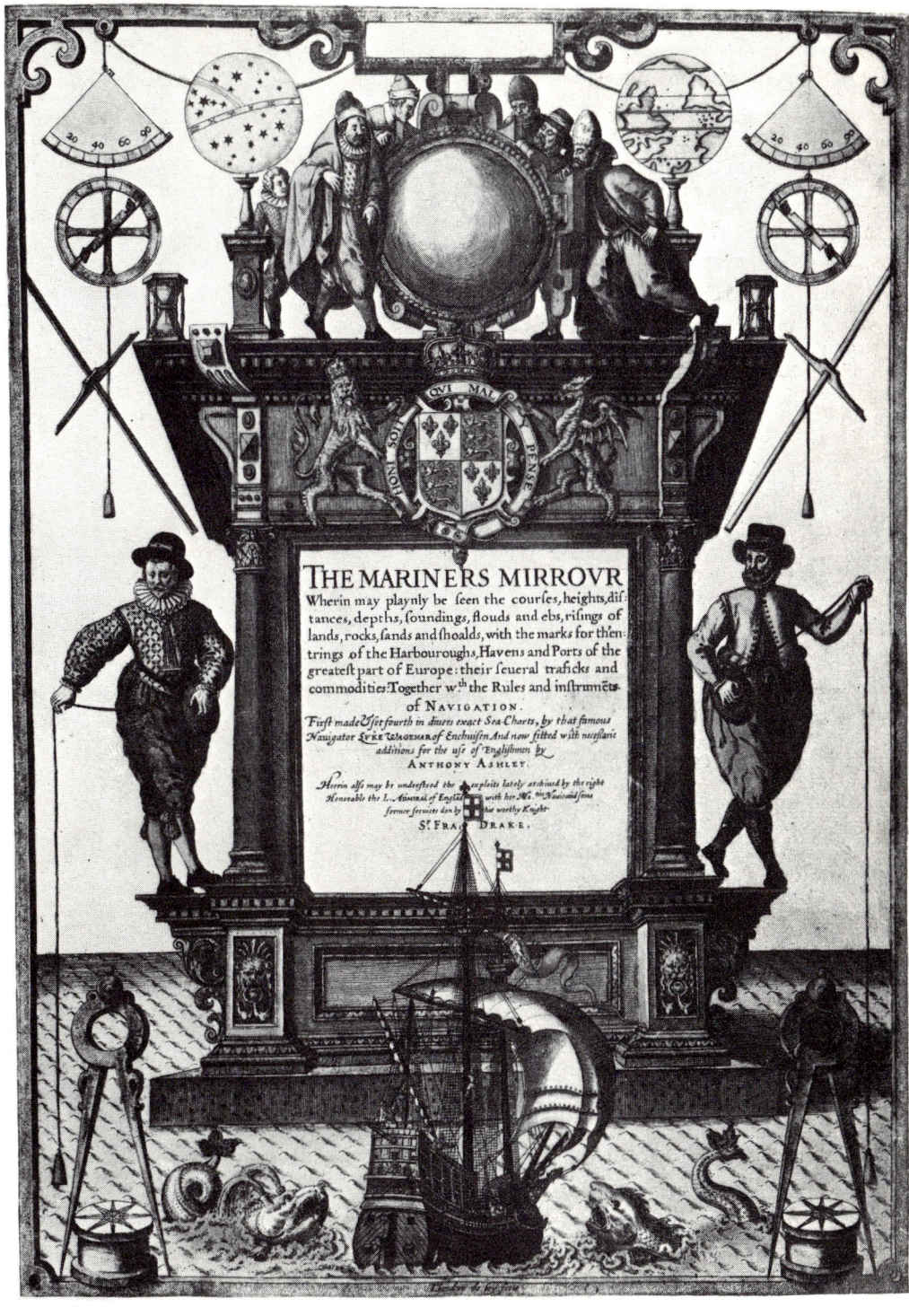

likely mutineer marks a momentous step in discipline afloat. He knew that defeat and disaster were the children of disobedience.

As a master of naval warfare, Drake's carefully planned combined operations on the strongholds of the Spanish Main were even more remarkable than his captures of prizes. But there was so much more to the man than the successful, rumbustious seadog, eager for plundered treasure. His Protestantism burned as intensely as his patriotism. 'This our captain was a religious man towards God and his houses,' wrote one who knew him well, 'generally sparing churches where he came, chaste in his life, just in his dealings, true to his word, and merciful to those who came under him, hating nothing so much as idleness.' A child of the English Bible, he could never forget the tragedy of Queen Mary's reign, epitomized in Fox's *Book of Martyrs,* and never forgave the Spaniards for the cruelties of the Inquisition from which so many of his shipmates suffered; and yet the Captain who dined to the music of viols was no straight-laced Puritan. Francis Drake was the greatest seaman of the age during which England became established as the foremost maritime power and by his achievements and his inspiration was the principal architect of this supremacy. His place in the select band of national heroes is secure.

Another Armada medal: Drake was probably remembered best for his inspired strategy leading to the defeat of the Spanish.

Further Reading

Biographies: The most authoritative study is Sir Julian Corbett's *Drake and the Tudor Navy* (1898, 2 volumes) which is much more than a biography. More recent publications are J.A. Williamson, *The Age of Drake* (1938); K.R. Andrews, *Drake's Voyages* (1967); Hans P. Kraus, *Sir Francis Drake* (1970) and George Malcolm Thomson, *Sir Francis Drake* (1972). Lady Elliott-Drake, *The Family and Heirs of Sir Francis Drake* (1911, volume 1) has many interesting sidelights.

General: Of a host of titles, the most readable are: A.L. Rowse, *The Expansion of Elizabethan England* (1955); C.M. Haring, *The Spanish Empire* (1941); A.P. Newton, *The European Nations in the West Indies* (1936); J.H. Parry, *The Age of Reconnaissance* (1963) and F. Braudel, *The Mediterranean World in the Age of Philip II* (1949, English translation 1972). All contain full bibliographies.

Discovery and Seamanship: E.G.R. Taylor, *Late Tudor – Early Stuart Geography* (1934); D.W. Waters, *The Art of Navigation in Elizabethan England and Early Stuart Times* (1958) and Gregory Robinson, *The Elizabethan Ship* (1956) are helpful guides to these topics. The pages of *The Mariner's Mirror,* the journal of the Society for Nautical Research, contain a great many articles on a wide range of subjects.

Campaigns and Voyages: Many of the publications of the Hakluyt Society are devoted to editions of texts relating to English maritime enterprise in the age of Drake. These supplement R. Hakluyt's *The Principal Navigations* of 1589, of which the best edition is that by W. Raleigh (1903–5, 12 volumes). John Hampden, *Francis Drake, Privateer* (1972) provides a useful commentary to the contemporary narratives and documents which he reprints. J.A.K. Laughton's *State Papers relating to the Defeat of the Armada* (Navy Record Society, 1894, 2 volumes) throws much light on Drake during the Armada campaign. Garrett Mattingly, *The Defeat of the Spanish Armada* (1959), is full of insight and written with great verve.

Contemporaries: See in particular J.A. Williamson, *Hawkins of Plymouth* (1949); Rayner Unwin, *The Defeat of Sir John Hawkins* (1960); Michael Lewis, *The Hawkins Dynasty* (1969); A.L. Rowse, *Sir Richard Grenville of the Revenge* (1937); Neville Williams, *Elizabeth I Queen of England* (1967); E. St John Brook, *Sir Christopher Hatton* (1946) and William M. Wallace, *Sir Walter Raleigh* (1959).

List of Illustrations

2 Sir Francis Drake, *National Portrait Gallery*.
3 Sir Francis Drake, Nicholas Hilliard, *National Maritime Museum*.
10–11 Edward VI and Pope, *National Portrait Gallery*
12 Francis Drake, *Archiv Gerstenberg*
13 Russell, 1st Earl, *National Portrait Gallery*
14–15 Map of Plymouth, *British Museum*
15 Fox, *National Portrait Gallery*
15 Sir Thomas Wyatt, *National Portrait Gallery*
18 Map of the World, beginning of 15th Century, photograph JOHN FREEMAN, *British Museum*
20 Eastern Hemisphere, photograph JOHN FREEMAN, *British Museum*
21 Western Hemisphere, photograph JOHN FREEMAN, *British Museum*
24 Mary I and Philip of Spain, attributed to Hans Eworth, photograph ELSAM, MANN & COOPER, by kind permission of the Duke of Bedford
26 Ferdinand Magellan, *Archiv Gerstenberg*,
   Contemporary portrait of Copernicus, photograph DEREK WITTY, *Royal Society*
27 Vasco da Gama, *British Museum*
28 Sir John Hawkins, photograph TOM MOLLAND, *City Museum, Plymouth*
30–1 Map of the New World, 1545, *Archiv Gerstenberg*
34 The Plea Roll of Court of Queen's Bench, *Public Record Office, London*
36 West African tribes, by Levinius Hulsius, photograph RODNEY TODD-WHITE, *National Maritime Museum*
37 Map of Mediterranean and Africa
38 Natives dancing and preparing food, photograph JOHN FREEMAN, *British Museum*
39 Natives bringing fish to Europeans, photograph JOHN FREEMAN, *British Museum*
40 Observation of passage of the sun with astrolabe and cross-staff, 1557, *Radio Times Hulton Picture Library*
42–3 Ship on left: 'Jesus of Lübeck', *Pepys Collection, Magdalene College, Cambridge*
46–7 Map 1, *Design Practitioners Limited*
48 Compass design from Spanish map of 1582, by Juan Martinez, Arsenal Library, Paris, *Mansell Collection*
   The Navigator, by Stradanus, *Radio Times Hulton Picture Library*
49 Astrolabe made for Drake by Humphrey Cole, *National Maritime Museum*
   Moveable compass for the stars, from Wagener, *The Mariners Mirrour*, photograph A. C. COOPER, *Map Room, British Museum*
52–3 Spanish Galleons in mid-sixteenth-century, *Radio Times Hulton Picture Library*
54 Lord Burghley riding his mule in his garden, *Bodleian Library, Oxford*
56 John Dee, photograph JOHN FREEMAN, *British Museum*
57 Dee's *Art of Navigation*, *Bodleian Library, Oxford*
58 Breaming a ship, detail of woodcut from *Peregrinationes in Terram Sanctam*, photograph JOHN FREEMAN, *British Museum*
60 Francis Drake, *Radio Times Hulton Picture Library*

64–5 Map of central and South America, 1592, photograph JOHN FREEMAN, *British Museum*
69 Callao (Lima's Port) under attack from Dutch, by Levinius Hulsius, photograph RODNEY TODD-WHITE, *National Maritime Museum*
70 Walter, Earl of Essex, *National Portrait Gallery*
72–3 The English in Ireland, *British Museum*
72–3 Map of Irish campaign, *British Museum*
75 Sir Francis Walsingham after de Critz the Elder, *National Portrait Gallery*
76 Sir Christopher Hatton, *Northampton Museum*
78–9 Map on silver from Mercator World Map, *British Museum*
81 Shipwrights, *Pepys Collection, BPC Picture Library*
81 Diagram of ship, *Pepys Collection, Magdalene College, Cambridge*
82 Cornelius Ketel, Sir Martin Frobisher, *Bodleian Library, Oxford*
84 Hatton's Arms, photograph A.C. COOPER, *Northampton Art Gallery*
88 Maio, Cape Verde Islands, *British Museum*
89 Fish with insert map of West Africa, *British Museum*
90 Southern end of South America and Elizabeth Island, *British Museum*
93 Drake's attack on San Domingo, photograph RODNEY TODD-WHITE, *National Maritime Museum*
93 Drake's attack on Cartagena, photograph RODNEY TODD-WHITE, *National Maritime Museum*
96 Drake's attack on Santiago, photograph RODNEY TODD-WHITE, *National Maritime Museum*
98–9 Drake's circumnavigation, from De Bry, *Grand Voyages, National Maritime Museum*
100 The Giants' Musical Instruments and other sketches by Francis Fletcher, *Sloane Collection, British Museum*
101 Mucho Insula, *British Museum*
102 'The Burning Island', *British Museum*
102–3 Duck-like foule, *British Museum*
102–3 'Ye boats', *British Museum*
103 A frozen mountain, *British Museum*
104 The *Cacafuego* and the *Golden Hind*, *Archiv Gerstenberg*
108–9 Map 2, *Design Practitioners Limited*
112–3 Drake in California, *National Maritime Museum*
113 Drake's inscription in New Albion, *Bancroft Library, University of California*
113 Drake in New Albion, *National Maritime Museum*
115 Drake at Ternate before the Sultan, *National Maritime Museum*
116 *Golden Hind* on the rocks off Celebes, *London Library*
118–9 Lisbon, 1580, *National Maritime Museum*
121 Drake, photograph A.C. COOPER, *Print Room, British Museum*
122 Cascaes, 1580, *National Maritime Museum*
126 Cup given to Drake by Elizabeth to encase the coconut he brought her, photograph ROBERT CHAPMAN, *City Museum, Plymouth*
127 Queen Elizabeth knighting Drake at Deptford, 1580, *Radio Times Hulton Picture Library*
128 Drake's Seal, *Radio Times Hulton Picture Library*
130 Buckland Abbey, Devon, *Radio Times Hulton Picture Library*
131 Buckland Abbey, photograph ROBERT CHAPMAN, *City Museum, Plymouth*
131 Drake's Arms, photograph ROBERT CHAPMAN, *City Museum, Plymouth*
134 Elizabeth Sydenham, Lady Drake, *National Maritime Museum*
137 Raleigh, *National Portrait Gallery*
138–9 Map of the Americas, photograph JOHN FREEMAN, *British Museum*

140 Sir Richard Grenville, *National Portrait Gallery*
142–3 Map showing the Americas, Africa and Europe, photograph RODNEY TODD-WHITE, *National Maritime Museum*
144 Raid on St Augustine, photograph RODNEY TODD-WHITE, *National Maritime Museum*
146–7 Cadiz, 1580, *National Maritime Museum*
149 Francis Drake, *National Portrait Gallery*
150 Santa Cruz, *Museo Navale, Madrid*
152 Nottingham, *National Portrait Gallery*
154–5 Golden Lion, Armada, 1588, *Radio Times Hulton Picture Library*
157 Charles Howard of Effingham by Cockson, photograph A.C. COOPER, *British Museum*
158 Cadiz, *National Maritime Museum*
162–3 Portuguese sailing ship, *Radio Times Hulton Picture Library*
165 View of Lisbon including India House, photograph JOHN FREEMAN, *British Museum*
166–7 John Pine's views of the Armada, *National Maritime Museum*
168 The Duke of Medina-Sidonia, *Museo Navale, Madrid*
170–1 Armada ships, *Worshipful Society of Apothecaries*
174–5 The *Ark Royal, Radio Times Hulton Picture Library.*
176 Spanish Armada in the English Channel, tapestry by Pine, *Radio Times Hulton Picture Library*
177 English and Spanish fleets engaging near Plymouth, photograph A.C. COOPER, *Map Room, British Museum*
178 Extract from the *English Mercurie,* 1588, *Radio Times Hulton Picture Library*
179 'General Ship' of Andalusian Squadron taken to Torbay by Drake, 1588, *Radio Times Hulton Picture Library*
180–1 Armada off the Isle of Wight, *National Maritime Museum*
182 Philip II, painting by A. Sanchez Coello, *Scala*
182–3 Elizabeth, Armada portrait, *Woburn Abbey*
184 Spanish Armada, *Radio Times Hulton Picture Library*
185 Signatures of victorious English Admirals after defeat of Armada, *Radio Times Hulton Picture Library*
188–9 John Pine's views of the Spanish Armada, *National Maritime Museum*
190–1 John Pine's views of the Spanish Armada, *National Maritime Museum*
192–3 John Pine's views of the Spanish Armada, *National Maritime Museum*
197 Spanish Armada, *Scheepvaart Museum, Amsterdam*
198 Sir John Norris, *Hawkley Studio Associates Ltd.*
202–3 Armada Map, *National Maritime Museum*
204–5 Drake's chest showing *Golden Hind, Berkeley Castle, Gloucestershire*
207 Queen Elizabeth I, *Archiv Gerstenberg*
208 Sir Martin Frobisher, *National Maritime Museum*
213 Richard Drake, *National Maritime Museum*
214–5 Map of London by Braun and Hogenberg, *Guildhall*
216–7 Drake's compass on Plymouth Hoe, photograph ROBERT CHAPMAN, *City Museum, Plymouth*
222 Statue of Drake at Plymouth, *Radio Times Hulton Picture Library*
223 Drake's drum, photograph TOM MOLLAND, *City Museum, Plymouth*
223 *Golden Hind,* photograph ROBERT CHAPMAN, *City Museum, Plymouth*
224 *The Mariners Mirrour,* by Wagener, photograph A.C. COOPER, *Map Room, British Museum*
226 A Dutch medal, *National Maritime Museum*

Index

Alençon, Francis, Duke of, 120, 122, 125, 127 133
Antilles and Lesser Antilles, 44, 141, 218–9
Ark, 169, 172–3, 184, 194
Armada,
  threat from, 148–53, 156, 169;
  Drake cripples in Spain, 158–63;
  in English Channel, 169, 176–87
Azores, 163, 208–10

Baskerville, Sir Thomas, 217, 218–21
Borough, William, 153, 158–61
Bristol, Treaty of, 77
Buckland Abbey, 128–9, 132, 206
Burghley, Lord Treasurer, 55, 83, 91
Burrough, Sir John, 209

Cabot, John, 35
Cabot, Sebastian, 35
Cacafuego, 101, 104–5
Cadiz, 158–60, 221
Canaries, 66, 136, 141, 218
Cape of Good Hope, 117
Cape Horn, 95
Cape Verde Islands, 40, 44, 88, 141
Caribbean, *see* West Indies
Carleill, Christopher, 136, 141
Cartagena, 46, 67, 71, 141, 219
Castellanos, Miguel de, 41, 45–6
Catholicism, 17, 23, 74, 120, 122
Celebes, 111, 114
Chagres River, 59, 67–8
Chatham Chest, 195, 212
Cimaroons, 59, 67–71
Circumnavigation,
  plans for, 80–7;
  route:
  Atlantic Ocean, 87–91;
  South America, 91–104;
  Central America, 104–7;
  North America, 110–1;
  Pacific Ocean, 111–4;
  Indian Ocean, 114–7;
  Africa, 117;
  Plymouth, 117, 120
Corunna, 173, 200, 206

Davis, John, 135
Davis, Strait, 135
Devereux, Robert, 2nd Earl of Essex, 201, 206, 221
Devereux, Walter, 1st Earl of Essex, 74, 77
Doldrums, 91
Dominica, 44
Doughty, John, 132
Doughty, Thomas, 77, 83, 91–4, 107, 132
Drake, Edmund, 12–3, 16–9, 22, 23, 29, 41
Drake, Sir Francis,
  appearance, 80;
  character, 94, 106–7, 145, 179, 196;
  childhood, 12, 19, 22–3;
  civic concern for Plymouth, 129, 206–7;
  death, 220;
  discoveries, 95, 110;
  exploits, *see* circumnavigation, military/naval operations, Panama and privateering;
  homes, 128–9, 132, 197, 199, 206;
  injuries, 63, 68, 97;
  knighted, 125, 127;
  Member of Parliament, 133, 212;
  motives for exploits:
  national defence, 151, 199–200, 209–10;
  Protestantism, 164–5, 226;
obituary, 225–6;
plot to murder, 132;
and Queen Elizabeth, 80, 123–4, 172, 199, 209–10;
out of favour with, 123, 194, 206–7;
religion, *see* Protestant faith;
training in seamanship, 25, 29, 39, 58;
will, 211–3, 221;
wives .
  Mary (*née* Newman), 55–8, 120, 127, 129;
  Elizabeth (*née* Sydenham), 135, 221
Drake, Francis (of Esher), 211, 221
Drake, John, 41, 61, 62–3, 67, 95
Drake, Joseph, 41, 67
Drake, Richard (of Esher), 177, 211
Drake, Richard (of Plymouth), 19
Drake's Bay, 110
Drake's Island (St Nicholas's Island), 18

East India Company, 124
East Indies,
  in Drake's circumnavigation, 111–7;
  treasure from, 111, 163–4, 209
Elizabeth I, Queen of England,
  assassination, plans for, 133, 151;
  marriage conjecture;
  Alençon, Duke of, 120, 122, 125–7, 133;
  Philip II of Spain, 37;
Spanish hostilities:
  hope for settlement without force, 156, 168, 172;
  defence against Armada, 148, 153, 187, 194;
support for:
  Moluccas operation, 133;
  Panama attack, 211;
  Plate Fleet intervention, 207, 209, 212;
  Portugal Expedition, 199–201, 206;
  slave trading, 35;
  South American exploration, 85;
  wealth from Drake's raids, 124
Elizabeth Bonaventure, 136, 153, 158
Enriquez, Martin, Viceroy of Spain, 47, 51, 106
Essex, Earls of, *see* Devereux

Fire ships, 159–60, 184, 186
Fletcher, Francis, Chaplain, 114, 116–7
Fog, 91
Fox, John, 165, 226
Frobisher, Martin, 80, 122, 136, 176–7, 207–11

Gales, 46, 71, 85, 91, 95, 145, 158, 173, 186–7
Gilbert, Sir Humphrey, 122, 135
Gillingham, 19, 22–3
Golden Hind (Pelican), 85–8, 95, 125–8;
see also circumnavigation
Golden Lion, 153, 160–1
Gravelines, battle of, 186–94
Grenville, Sir Richard, 128–9, 135, 145, 208
Guadalupe, 218
Guatemala, 106–7

Hakluyt, Richard, 80, 135
Hatton, Christopher, 77, 80, 83, 95, 122, 133, 209
Hawkins, John,
  Armada, 168, 176;

231

Navy Treasurer, 32, 35, 80, 122, 133;
Plate Fleet:
  military/naval operation, 209, 212, 216–8;
  privateering, 39–41, 44–51, 55;
  slave trading, 29, 32, 35–7
Hawkins, Margery, mother of Francis Drake, 13, 22–3
Hawkins, Richard, 210
Hawkins, William, 32
Henry VIII, King of England, 16–7, 20, 32
Hispaniola, 19, 141
Howard, Lord Charles of Effingham, 169–75, 179, 185–7, 194–9
Howard, Lord Thomas, 208–11

Indian Ocean, 114, 117
Indians, Californian, 110–1
Indians, hostile, 97
Ireland, 74, 77, 122

Java, 117
Jesus of Lübeck, 44–50
Judith, 44–50, 55

Lane, Ralph, 135, 145
Leicester, Earl of, 80, 83, 133, 151, 187, 209

'Line', 35, 37, 51, 135
Lisbon, 163, 201
Lovell, Captain John, 39–41
Levant Company, 124, 153
Madre de Dios, 209
Magellan (Magalhães), Ferdinand, 87, 95
Mary, Queen of Scots, 23, 61, 122, 133, 151, 153
Medals, 196
Medina Sidonia, Duke of, 106, 168, 176, 179, 184, 186–7, 196
Medway, 23, 25
Mendoza, Don Bernardino de, 123, 125, 127, 133
Military/naval operations, see Armada, Ireland, Moluccas, Portugal Expedition, West Indies
Minion, 44–51

Moluccas, 111, 133, 135
Mule trains, raids on, 59, 68, 69
Mutiny, 91–2, 161, 210

Netherlands, 27–9, 37, 55, 61, 120, 133, 145, 148, 151
New Year gifts, 127–8, 132, 210
Nicaragua, 106
Nombre de Dios,
  privateering, 59, 62–6, 69,
  Drake's account, 210;
  military/naval operations, 219
Nonsuch, Treaty of, 148, 151
Norris, Sir John, 77, 199, 200
North West Passage, 36, 80, 109–10, 122, 135

Oxenham, John, 62, 63, 97, 101, 105

Pacific Ocean, 68, 80, 111–4
Panama, 59, 67–8, 211, 219
Papal bull, 35, 74, 148
Parma, Alexander Farnese, Prince of, 120, 133, 145, 148, 168–72, 184–7, 194
Patagonia, 92, 132
Pelican, see *Golden Hind*
Peru, 36, 97, 101
Philip II of Spain,
  claim to Portuguese throne, 120;
  'Enterprise', see Armada;
  and Elizabeth I, 37;
  and Mary Queen of Scots, 23, 36, 37;
  plot to kidnap Drake, 132;
  wealth: from East Indies, see *San Felipe*, from West Indies, see Plate Fleet
Plate Fleet, 36–9, 208, 218;
  interception, see privateering
Plymouth:
  Drake as citizen, 41, 77, 129, 206–7, 225;

Hawkins family home, 32, 44;
  plague in, 120;
  ships return to, 71, 74, 117, 120, 145, 221;
  Spanish ships incidents, 44, 55
Port Pheasant, 61–2
Port St Julian, 92–4
Port St Mary, 159
Portugal Expedition, 199, 200–1, 206
Privateering,
  small scale in English Channel, 19;
  in Spanish Main;
  Reneger, 19–21;
  Hawkins, William, 32;
  Hawkins, John, 35, 37;
  and Drake, 41–51, 213, 217–9;
  Drake, 58, 61–71, 144;
  Raleigh, 209
Protestant faith,
  Drake's, 12–3, 17, 41, 51, 77, 151;
  his devotions at sea, 106, 217;
  his motives for exploits, 164–5, 226;
  persecution of, 17–8, 23;
  and politics, 120, 122, 132–3, 196
Puerto Rico, 218–9

Raleigh, Sir Walter, 110, 133, 135, 206, 209
Ranse, James, 62–6
Rebellion, 17, 23
Recalde, Juan Martinez de, 160, 176
Reneger, Robert, 19–22
Revenge, 169, 176, 177, 195, 207, 209
Rio de la Hacha, 40–1, 45–6, 219
Rosario, 176, 194, 196

Sagres, 160–1
San Cristobel, 101
San Felipe, 163–4
San Juan de Ulua, 46–7, 50, 55, 107
San Salvador, 19
Santa Cruz, Marquis of, 158, 163, 168
Santa Marta, 46, 67, 136, 219
Seymour, Lord Henry, 169, 179, 194, 195

Sickness, 51, 67, 141, 144–5, 195, 201, 222
Silva, Nuño da, 85, 88–91, 95, 97, 107–8
Slave trading, 35, 39–41
South America, 85, 91–104
Spain,
  hostile to England, 80, 127, 133, 135, 148, see also Armada and Philip II;
  power of, 25, 61, 120;
  wealth from New World, see Plate Fleet and privateering
Swan, 58, 61, 62, 67, 87, 91, 92

Tagus River, 200–1
Tavistock, 12–3, 17
Ternate, 111
Thomas, 186
Trade winds, 111
Treasure:
  East Indies, 111, 163–4, 209;
  West Indies, see Mule trains, Nombre de Dios, Plate Fleet and San Juan de Ulua

Valdes, Don Pedro de, 176–7, 211
Vancouver Island, 110
Venezuela, 44–5
Venta Cruces, 68–9
Vera Cruz, 46, 50
Vigo, 136, 201
Virgin Islands, 218
Virginia, 111, 135, 145

Walsingham, Sir Francis, 77, 80, 83, 122, 133, 151, 172, 209
West Indies,
  in Drake's circumnavigation, 141;
  military/naval operations in, 135, 209, 212, 216–8;
  Spanish treasure in see treasure and privateering
Wynter, John, 87, 97
Wynter, Sir William, 32, 55, 58, 83

Zarate, Don Francisco de, 106, 107